# Stories From The Heart

## The Carers Journey

Created by

# Christine Stow

First published in 2023 through *We Inspire Now Books*, a business assisting authors to self-publish.

Copyright © 2023 Christine Stow

ISBNs
Print:    9780645825206
Ebook:   9780645825213

Christine Stow has asserted her right under the Copyright Act 1968 to be identified as the author of this work. The information in this book is based on each author's experiences and opinions. Each author retains copyright over their individual work.

Antoinette Pellegrini, through her business, *We Inspire Now Books*, specifically disclaims responsibility for any adverse consequences, which may result from the use of the information contained herein in the works by the other individual authors. Each individual author takes responsibility for their content and for any permissions to use information. Any breaches will be rectified in further editions of the book.

This work is copyright. Apart from any use permitted under the Copyright Act 1968, no part of this publication may be reproduced, stored in or introduced into a retrieval system, or transmitted in any form, or by any means (electronic, mechanical, photocopying, recording or otherwise) without the prior written permission of the author. Any person who commits any unauthorised act in relation to this publication may be liable to criminal prosecution and civil claims for damages. Enquiries should be made through We Inspire Now Books.

| | |
|---|---|
| **Cover image**: | www.unsplash.com |
| | kelly-sikkema-4le7k9XVYjE-unsplash |
| **Cover Design:** | Jessica Salzone |
| **Layout:** | Antoinette Pellegrini |
| | We Inspire Now Books |

We Inspire Now Books
PO BOX 133 Greensborough,
Victoria Australia 3088
www.weinspirenowbooks.com

# Dedication

This book is dedicated to my daughters.

Auraria, for making me a mother.

Imyjen, for making me a carer and taking me on this journey.

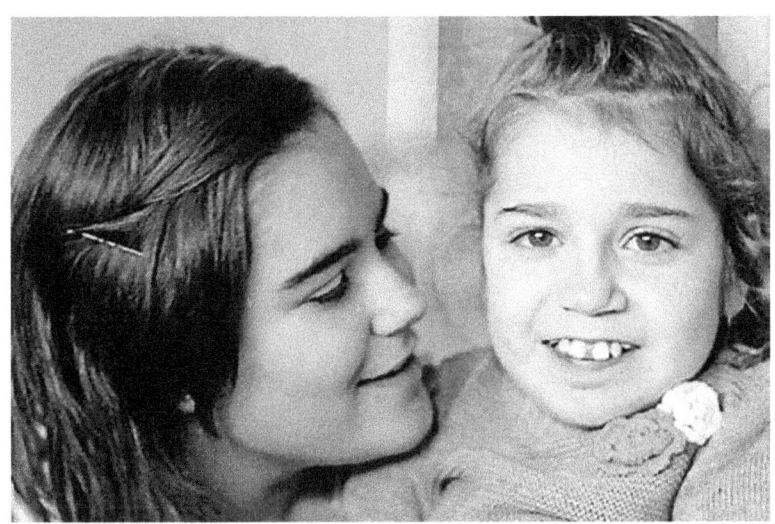

# Contents

| | | |
|---|---|---|
| Foreword | *Christine Stow* | 1 |
| Imyjen Is My Gift | *Christine Stow* | 7 |
| My Family's Journey | *Anastasia Searle* | 21 |
| The Gift of Learning, From Son To Mum | *Monique Peters* | 33 |
| Twins and Autism – A Life Changing Journey | *Jenny Nechvatal* | 43 |
| We Were Entrusted With A Child, Not A Syndrome: Justin | *Alessandra Pelletier* | 55 |
| Fostering Is For The Open Hearted | *Irina Castellano* | 65 |
| Let Go OF Guilt An Embrace Love | *Graciela Ramon Michel* | 77 |
| Our Boy Who Changes Our Lives | *Julie Fisher* | 91 |
| Life Is Mainly Froth And Bubbles | *Nicole Dunn* | 103 |
| Of Course Our Son Brought Us Joy. Why Wouldn't He? | *Lorraine Gaunt* | 113 |
| Life In The Fast Lane | *Chris Hill* | 123 |
| Author Bios | | 135 |

# Foreword
## Christine Stow

Soon after I published my story in 2015, I wanted to put together a book a compilation of stories of others who have walked a similar pathway

At the time I didn't know why I wanted to do it I just knew that I wanted to do it I just knew that I wanted to bring together a group of parents who are looking after their children with disabilities to share their stories.

My first book, *Not Just Imyjens Mother,* came about after I attended a book writing workshop. I'm not a writer or a reader, for that matter, and it was not something I aspired to do. But I was inspired to write my story at the workshop.

From there, we mapped out the outline, and I attended a weekend retreat to write the book. Wow! What a watershed that was! I had never left my daughter Imyjen for more than three hours before that, and here I was going away for a whole weekend!

Imyjen is a special gift. She's lit the pathway for me to see things differently and to DO things differently.

If not for her, I don't think I would have stood in a federal election, been elected to local government, stood in a state election, written a book, or met the people along the journey and made the friends that I have.

Maybe I would have.

Writing my own story put me on a pathway that I am forever grateful for. One where I have been able to inspire others. I have been invited to speak as a motivational speaker and have spoken to Members of Parliament and Disability Service Providers.

People now ask where they can buy my book. It lights up my soul when someone says, 'Because of your story, I was able to go on'.

I was inspired to publish a book of carers' stories, but I put it on the back burner for the time being, although it was always something I was going to do and always something that was going to happen.

I imagined that when I was ready to begin the journey to create my book of carers' stories, my friend would walk the journey with me. I had always imagined she would be part of this, and that she would write a chapter. But in March 2022, my friend suddenly passed away.

We had set up a support group when our children were very young. She was someone that I would say I had most shared my journey with. She knew my inner secrets. She knew the darkness and the light of the pathway we tread along the way to a 'diagnosis' for our beautiful children.

And now she was not going to be there to be part of this writing journey. I was heartbroken.

I questioned myself. How much longer was I going to put this off? What else was I going to wait for? Who else would not be here to be part of this journey?

My friend's passing gave me the inspiration, the energy, and the kick in the backside to make this happen NOW.

Now is the time.

When I first started to talk about this book to other carers who share this journey, I wasn't getting the kind of stories that I was looking for. This just made me question what is it I am looking for?

Maybe this is a lost cause?

Maybe it wasn't.

Through talking to people, it became clear to me that what I was looking for was for carers to be able to share their journey. As the title goes: *Stories From The Heart: The Carers Journey.*

But none of this would have become clear if I didn't start the journey with this book.

What I wanted is for people who participate in this book to be able to speak to other carers, to share their story, to share the inspiration, and to map out the pathway for others who are following, those who are new to caring either by illness or age or diagnosis. I also hoped that the authors themselves would benefit from the healing that you can get from writing your own story.

You see, people say they are inspired when I share my journey, when I share my story. That is what I want for the other authors.

It is so pleasing, inspiring and heartwarming to read the other authors' stories here. They all have their own individual stories to tell, yet all of them have expressed the same sentiment, that although caring for someone with a disability is tough, and that there will be tears, there is also joy and gratitude for what their child has brought to their lives.

So, although the journey may be a difficult one, there will be light at the end of the tunnel.

Each of the authors brings love and realness to their chapter. What I didn't expect, was the enlightenment that I got from reading the other chapters. I thought I knew how tough it was, or I thought I knew the authors well, but I didn't really. I didn't until I read their personal journeys, and I hope that the reader will be touched and inspired by their stories, as I was.

People have said to me, 'Because I read your book, because you shared your story, I was able to go on, I was able to step up and to achieve things I didn't think I could.'

THAT is what I want to create for others.

I decided to live the best life that I possibly could around Imyjen's needs. I figure that there's no point being sad, there's no point being depressed because that's not going to do Imyjen any good. That's what I want other carers to know, or others reading our stories: that many things are possible against seemingly impossible odds, if we think of new ways.

There are possibilities. It is possible to live the best life.

It takes a change in the way you look at things, and Imyjen allowed me to do that. It takes a different mindset. It takes changing things from impossibility to possibility.

I have created this book for people who are embarking on a similar journey as a carer, or maybe for people who have just found out there's something wrong with their child, or who have to deal with cancer or face some great challenge in their lives.

I want those who are reading this to know that there are possibilities, that there are other people who've walked the journey and have lived differently and achieved great things.

That's the essence of what I would like others to get out of this book:

You're not alone.

And can do it.

This is not the life that I've chosen; this is not the life that I imagined.

It's a different life.

It's not good.

It's not bad.

IT'S JUST A DIFFERENT LIFE.

# Imyjen Is My Gift

## Christine Stow

## My Life Changed

My life changed for me when I found out there was something wrong with my daughter. I remember sitting there after seeing the child and maternal health nurse, and my life just seemed to drift away before me, like the bottom had fallen out of my world.

I had worked so hard to get to where I was: to be a national sales manager in a medical supply company. My life was where I wanted it to be. I had the dream life, and all of a sudden, that was gone - taken it away from me.

My life felt like a merry-go-round that I could not get off. An endless cycle of doctors, appointments, health professionals, speech therapists, occupational therapists, phone calls, and social workers.

At one time, I counted 12 health professionals involved in her care, and she was only three months old! 'Go here. Do this. See this person. We don't know what it is. Maybe it's this. Maybe it's that'. And on it went It. I felt like I was in a world I did not belong in.

This was not my world.

Why me?

Why us?

Why my baby?

I made deals with God. I pleaded, 'Make her well. Make this go away.' But nothing changed. Nothing improved.

Therapists told me I wasn't working hard enough to get her to speak, operations, and surgery. It was so far and different from what I had imagined my life to be. The future looked bleak, and I fell into depression.

**Therapies and Diagnosis**

Imyjen was born in September. It was at the three-month child and maternal health check when the nurse turned to me uttering those words: 'She's not meeting her milestones.'

Next, I recall going to see a pediatrician. Then an orthopaedic surgeon. We were flung into this world just on Christmas. I visited this surgeon between Christmas and New Year. No one seemed to be around the hospital. It was cold and dark and grey, empty and gormless. Much seemed like that at the time.

The surgeon was lovely and friendly and all, but it felt cold, and I was lost.

He was looking at her hips. She was stiff, and the stiffness was pulling her bones, and her hips were out of place. They needed to be in place to grow properly.

You find out so many things when your child is not quite 'normal'.

The next pediatrician said, 'You will feel so much better when you get a diagnosis.' I didn't want a diagnosis; I wanted a normal child. My response was, 'What difference is it going to make? I'm still going to love her the same. She'll still be the same person.' I didn't want her to be just a diagnosis.

## Going Back to Work

I had planned to go back to work after having Imyjen. I had Care arranged, and it was all going to go just like with Auraria; put her into Care and off I would go to work, my big corporate gig.

My manager called me to organise to go back to work. I had to explain to him that there was something wrong with my beautiful baby and that I couldn't go back to work. There was no way I could see how I was going to be able to manage working and caring for my baby. I 'didn't know what the outcome would be for her. I didn't know what her diagnosis was, and we didn't know what her prognosis would be.

It was made all that much harder because he and his wife had children roughly the same time as us. There were so many tough points to navigate.

## Time for Surgery

As a baby, Imyjen had to endure many surgeries, not knowing what was going on. I didn't know how to cope. I was encouraged to enrol her in chi by the allied health workers. I didn't know what I was doing. I just blindly followed the social workers' advice.

I had organised Care for my first daughter, Auraria, so I could go back to work when she was six months old. It was hard to let go of my baby then, but I was ready to return to work. I'd seen myself as always working. Indeed, I used to say, 'I am not sure I will put the bottle in the right end: I just don't know about babies.' It's incredible how you just know once the baby arrives.

In contrast, finding something wrong with Imyjen was just a haze, especially not knowing where to go or how to deal with this. Finally, I got Imyjen into childcare two days a week. I think back and wonder what on Earth I was thinking.

She had been glued to my hip for 18 months, not the six months like with Auraria. We had been on a journey, a tough journey. Finding child care was so much harder, and so was letting go. I drove around and around in circles that morning. Lost. Not knowing what to do with myself.

As time went on, it became clear that Imyjen 'not meeting her milestones' meant more - a whole lot more. Her hips were out of place and her hands were bent up. She needed surgery to 'fix' these things

Then the cavalry arrived in the form of my sister-in-laws from Queensland. They were a godsend and cared for Auraria while I was in the hospital with Imyjen. They cleaned the house, they cleaned the floor, and they cleaned all the clothes! Things that I had and were sacred to me, I found in the bin. My (now ex) husband said, 'They even stole the dust from under our couch!' Whilst I felt a bit put out by their cleaning methods, they were a Godsend at a tough time.

It was hard handing over my tiny baby with the twisted legs, who we did not know what was wrong with, to a doctor to perform surgery on. You can explain it to a child or an adult - but not a tiny precious baby. We had to have faith.

After the surgery, Imyjen was in a plaster cast from chest to legs with just an opening for the nappy. It was a challenging time, but we got through. Though she was heavy, the upside was that she was kind of like a board rather than a baby that flops around. And there were no baths for the six weeks she was in plaster.

After the surgery, the doctor said, 'I have good news and bad news. The surgery was a success, but now I have to do the other side.' And we did it all over again.

**We are a Whole Family**

From the time we found out something was wrong with Imyjen, I was doing all I could to get the best for our family. We were provided with support in the form of HACC (Home and Community Care). That was helpful, but there were many rules. It could only be for Imyjen, not for our other daughter. Many times I needed my other daughter cared for while I was visiting the many doctors and allied health services. Auraria was dragged around, made to sit through therapies with snack packs and dollies that didn't always keep her amused.

She could say physiotherapist and orthopaedic surgeon before she could say our address! What I needed was support for Auraria to get us through this, not just Imyjen. We are a whole family - not just the family of one child with disabilities.

## Supports

Early on, I attended a support group for parents of children with special needs. I remember looking at other parents in awe. They were working around their children's care, and I thought, 'That will never be me.'

Once Imyjen was in child care, which I was doing because I was assured it was good for her, she got to socialise with other children. She sat at the table with other children who were feeding themselves. She was curious and wanted to do that too. To the point where she would reach over other children and take some of their food!

One day the centre staff said to me: 'Wow, Imyjen really likes those biscuits!' I almost fainted because I had only given her thick food. I was protecting her from choking on biscuits. Maybe I was just protecting her from my own fears.

We were introduced to Interchange. This is where a family takes the child for a weekend or day to give the caring family a break. Our family was a God send. We still consider them family 20 years later.

In one of the first outings, the mum came over to pick Imyjen up to take her for the day while I spent time with Auraria. As she drove away with my precious babe, Auraria sat on the seat out front of our house crying, 'That's MY sister. Where is she taking my sister? That's MY sister.' It brings tears to my eyes even now. We don't often consider or understand how the disability affects the siblings or how they see it. Auraria has always been, and even to this day, very interactive and protective of her sister.

From here, I was able to get a casual role at the hospital as a ward clerk. It was at least something that I could do and feel I was contributing, but I always felt that I was not appreciated for what I could really offer, having been a National Technical Adviser for Medical Products – now I had no value.

**Learning about Disability Services**

Given Imyjen's care needs, we moved across town to be closer to my parents, who could offer support for us as a family and care for Auraria more easily while I was attending appointments.

At this time, a job was advertised for Coordinator Northern Region Disability Network. I'd always been a networker and ran events as the social club secretary at Forensic Science and a Chromatography group in

Brisbane. I thought this would be easy for me and attractive because I would learn about disability services.

I went to the interview. This was big for me; getting back into regular work while caring for Imyjen. Yep! I know. I never thought it would be possible, but now I wanted to make it real.

In the first instance, I was rejected because I didn't have formal disability training. I was 'only a carer', and that didn't count toward experience in disability.

As fate would have it, the preferred nominee rejected the offer, and I was in! I took on the role and learnt a lot, met a lot of people, and they learnt from me. After some time in this role, my manager said to me, 'You are really good at this.' I thanked him and said, 'Yes, it's not the disability experience that makes me good at this. It's my previous experience in sales that make me good at this'.

We all have transferable skills that we can apply in new situations. I went on to use my transferable skills to write a program to help small businesses and not-for-profits write and apply for grants. I used what I had learnt in applying for a grant myself and seeing it from the other side as a Councillor.

**Political Life**

Around that time, some people set up a political party to lobby for what is now NDIS (National Disability Insurance Scheme). They asked me to stand for them since I had connections with a wide range of the disability community: service providers, carers and people with disabilities.

I remember having a discussion with Brad about what that would mean to us as a family. It was a hard call since we didn't know anything about politics. We decided to do it, and he was totally on board and supported me.

This experience taught me that anything is possible when you put your mind to it- that if you believe it can be done - then it can. I met a lot of people and got even more understanding of disability services which opened up a new world to me. I believe I would have ever stood in any election if not for finding something wrong with Imyjen. I might have, but I more likely would have stayed on my previous career trajectory. I might have ended up with more significant titles, or I might have even been made redundant. That's never going to happen caring for Imyjen!

We 'didn't get elected, but we did make an impact; we made a difference. I learnt that it's important to have someone sitting at the table - the big table - the parliamentary table. For all the lobbying and writing letters, it was not until we stood for something that we were listened to. We need more carers in important roles so that we can influence the decisions.

Next, I was asked to stand in the local government election. At the time, I was newly single. I didn't stand a chance, or so I thought. I did all I could working around Imyjen's care. I got elected. It was a shock I felt that the people had asked me to be their representative. I decided that I would do what I could to make it work. There were big changes for me to make about how I cared for Imyjen. I had to work out what I HAD to do and what I could delegate. That was a steep learning curve.

I am very proud of what I achieved as Councilor: A special school, a cafe for people with disabilities and an NDIS forum for carers to understand what it would mean as it rolled into our area.

**Reflections**

Having Imyjen as my second child was going to complete my family. I had the corporate life, the two cars, the two company cars, and this was going to be easy. I was going to relax and enjoy both of my children as babies at home together

For a time, I did until that child and maternal health nurse uttered those words, and my life spun out of control.

Imyjen has taken me on a journey, a different journey than what I expected, a different journey to the one that I dreamed of as the ideal life in my head.

I now realise that Imyjen made me look at things differently. She has given me the opportunity to stop and smell the roses, to do things differently. WHO KNOWS, maybe I might have been out of control in a corporate career.

In the beginning, I cried out, asking God, 'Why me? This wasn't meant to be me. I'm not tough; I'm not strong. I can't do this.'

Then I stood in the state election, in the local government election and federal election. I realised it WAS MEANT to be me. I was meant to speak for people with disabilities and carers. I was put in this position, and Imyjen has just given me a different roadmap, a different pathway, a pathway that I now cherish.

She put me in front of different people, people who I would never have met, never have imagined in my life, but people I have developed friendships with.

After my ex left, I saw a counsellor. I had suffered anxiety and depression early in the journey, and I wanted to check that I was okay. After a while, I thought I wanted to go back to work, and I told her that. She said to me, 'You're a carer. That's why you get the carer's pension.'

I thanked her, and I walked that day saying to myself, 'I will find somebody who believes that I can, not somebody who says that I can't. From there, I went on to find mentors and coaches who believed in me. We mapped out pathways and made it happen.

Oprah Winfrey, Tony Robbins and JK Rowling all came from difficult circumstances to overcome challenges. You can say, 'Sure, but they've got there. They are millionaires.' But their lives were very tough at some stage. They overcame challenges, and that's what I want others to believe, others who come from a similar position to me, to believe in what is possible.

There's gotta be an upside, and of course, there are times when I take advantage of the situation; where I use Imyjen's disability as an excuse. 'Sorry, I can't get a carer,' when really I don't want to go out, or I don't want to do those things. I don't tell anyone. It's just a little secret, okay? Shhhh!

Things might take a little bit longer, but they are possible. I mean standing in the state election, writing my book, and completing my Masters of Business Administration all since finding something wrong with Imyjen. It's possible if you put your mind to it. I even got Dux of my Strategic Management Class of my MBA because the life experience gained caring for Imyjen makes everything make so much more sense.

As hard or as difficult as it is, I won't be defined by Imyjen's disabilities. I'm not just Imyjens mama, I'm much much more.

I want other carers, and other people facing challenges to know that it is possible to look at the examples of others who have trod the path and achieved great things.

Most of all, if you're reading this, I want you to believe in yourself, to believe that it's possible you can achieve things. My hope is that you, like me, won't be defined by the disability but be defined by a determination to achieve something. Set your dreams and set about making them happen.

# My Family's Journey

## Anastasia Searle

For me, there seemed to be two parallel journeys in relation to my daughter's disability. The 'outer' journey charted the difficulties and the reality of what we as a family had to physically face and do, whist the second was the 'inner' journey, the journey that involved learning about disability, understanding a new mindset, and witnessing how I changed as a person along the way. That inner journey became my saving grace and helped me keep our family balanced during challenging times.

**A Father's Journey**

It was when Jaqueline was a baby, and her milestones were behind for her age, that my husband Angus and I first felt that something was not quite right. Even so, when I found out that my daughter had autism and an intellectual disability, I was heartbroken.

Heartbreak quickly turned into denial, which lasted a number of years. Angus, who had grown up with a sister who had a disability, approached the situation with a lot of wisdom and a deeper, first-hand knowledge. Angus told me to just love Jaqueline and to be her mother rather than exhaust myself attending ongoing appointments that may not be necessary, trying to do so much more than was needed. So, I did the essential and not the impossible.

What Angus suggested made a lot of sense and was very helpful when it came to the decisions that we needed to make. His wisdom helped me to be calmer, happier and to enjoy our daughter and family life, and to let her older brother and sister (my stepchildren) just love her too.

As Jaqueline became older, her behaviour started becoming difficult, and her support needs changed. It was a very challenging time, and I was at a loss about what to do. Again, Angus and his wisdom came to the fore. He said he thought it was time for us to move forward and to look at what Jaqueline's future needs would be.

Although we'd always had help, it was mostly medical attention, and what we needed to do now was to dive deep and find the emotional and social support that Jaqueline really needed to equip her for the future. We also wanted to explore any other therapies that were not purely medical that might help Jaqueline.

Unlike today with the NDIS and the many other services available to people with a disability and their families, there were fewer resources available back then. The available resources were not always easy to find or even know about their existence – at least, that was our experience. Just trying to find support and resources to help with Jaqueline's development consumed most of my time and energy.

When we were trying to decide what school to enrol Jaqueline at, I found that mainstream schools had some supports for children with disabilities, and I had my heart set on one particular school. Angus instinctively felt that Jaqueline should go to a special school. Looking back now at all the research I did concerning finding the right school for our daughter, I can see his fatherly instincts were correct. I would've done things differently, but I trusted in his instincts and his wisdom, so Jaqueline attended a special school for 15 years until she graduated in 2021.

When we were deciding what school Jaqueline should attend, we didn't know the difficulties ahead of us because we had yet to experience her extremely challenging behaviour. I can see now how incredibly difficult it would have been for everyone involved – especially for Jaqueline herself – if she had attended a mainstream school that could not provide the right supports to manage her extreme behaviours.

Fortunately, over the years, with lots of research, learning, and interventions via specialists and allied health professionals, and I suspect Jaqueline just getting older, her challenging behaviours are now very rare, and she has a much happier and loving personality.

Angus has always been a very involved parent with all of his children, whether it's doing the physical work of parenting or teaching them from his life experience, and he has always been openly affectionate with them. Thank goodness for this and for our united approach, as sometimes (even now) caring for Jaqueline can still take both of us.

Angus's approach to parenting, coupled with his fatherly knowing, has allowed him to create a strong bond with his children, and he has been a solid role model for his older children (my stepchildren) in relation to disability. Even when they were younger, Jaqueline's siblings, Emily and Austin, often stepped into the 'young carer' role with enthusiasm, no matter how challenging it may have been. They are adults now, and both have worked as support workers at different times over the past few years with various clients, but with already a lifetime of first-hand experience behind them.

## A Mother's Journey

I suspect that my judgement in deciding the best options for Jaqueline was clouded by my denial, which I guess is both part of the grieving process and my hope at the time that she would grow out of her difficulties. Once I emerged from the denial stage, many things changed. I was able to trust in my instincts as a mother and to know that, in addition to a lot of research on my part, I would always know what was best for my family.

Meeting Jaqueline's constant needs and demands interfered with other relationships as it was difficult to connect with family and friends and be able to do the things that interested us. We could not go out as there were very few people who could look after our daughter.

My mother had always loved looking after Jaqueline, but eventually, when my mother became elderly, I had to stop leaving Jaqueline with her at her home. One day, about an hour later after I had dropped Jaqueline at my mother's, I felt a very strong urge to return to my mother's home early.

When I arrived, all the doors were open and no one was at home. I knew immediately that something was wrong. I drove around the streets until I found them heading home. I later found out that my daughter had left the house and my elderly mother had chased her across a main road, with Jaqueline disappearing into a large park. Eventually, my mother found her, but by then, stressed and exhausted, she still had to coax Jaqueline to walk back home with her, which was the point at which I found them. I decided that day that as much as I needed the support and time out, I could not put my mother in that situation again.

## The Siblings' Journey

Often, when Jaqueline exhibited challenging behaviours, Austin would come out of his room to help. Austin was in his mid-teens, and Jaqueline was five years younger. However, Austin's presence always seemed to stop Jaqueline in her tracks. No matter what behaviour she was exhibiting, she would stop, look at him and then totally cooperate.

I could have made a small fortune if I'd known how he was able to instantly transform her just with his presence! And Emily and Jaqueline have a love that makes me believe they are soulmates, which is something I never associated with siblings. As they have grown older (both are now in their twenties), the affection, sharing and laughter continues.

## Making Time for Us

With my daughter's 24/7 support requirements, my relationships with my husband and stepchildren could have fallen apart. The journey was extremely difficult, and sometimes I was so exhausted it felt like every part of my body ached. Other times, I could not keep my eyes open, having been up all through the night taking care of Jaqueline's complex needs.

I could barely function from the extreme exhaustion. Somewhere in all this chaos of life, I knew it was important to make our relationship a priority because I knew this journey would either make us all or break us all. To keep our relationship healthy and happy, my husband

and I realised that we needed to make it a priority, and I took 100 per cent responsibility for helping it happen.

So, despite the challenges, making my husband a priority and making time for us to spend together enjoying good things and to talk and laugh, became extremely important. We would go for walks around the block, and the rule was no talking about problems during the walks.

At times, I would have to put my husband and myself first to make sure that I had that time with my husband, and, as a result, we have a happy married life. Since making this decision, the challenges with Jaqueline seem a bit less stressful. Despite her not always being the top priority, she's happy, and it's as if she's happy because *we* are happy.

It was also important that my stepchildren's needs were taken care of when they were children, and, as a result of doing this, they are now well-adjusted adults. Although they have since moved out to live their own lives, we continue to have a close family bond. They love their sister. But I think it could've been a different story had I allowed the challenges of the outer journey with its difficulties and the exhaustion to take over instead and then neglected to build those close family bonds with them.

When it comes to extended family and friends, I suppose that very little is able to be understood by them about the challenges socialising creates when you have a child with a disability. We rarely got to attend social functions, but when Jaqueline was about nine, there was a family wedding that we really wanted to attend. I managed to get some funding (this was before the NDIS) for a carer to support Jaqueline so we could go to the wedding. While at the wedding reception, my husband got a call from the agency, saying that the carer was struggling with Jaqueline and could we go home. I was so deeply upset by this request that I took the phone and gave the carer some instructions. To be honest, I was quite forceful; however, the carer did decide to stay.

## Coming to Terms with the Term 'Carer'

The word 'carer' is used in relation to the family that supports or raises a child with a disability. I feel strongly that I am NOT a carer, but that I am a mother who has raised a daughter who just happens to have a disability.

When people talked about a carer, I would only think of the support workers who came into my home and helped my daughter, not myself. I remember the first time that I realised that when they mentioned carers, they were actually talking about me, and I was horrified! As far as I was concerned, I was a mother, and while my daughter had certain needs that were probably significantly more challenging than most other children her age, I still felt that my role was that of a mother taking care of her child. I have since made my peace with the term 'carer', acknowledging now that my perception of it is not everyone else's.

## How Was This Possible? My Career Journey

Disability is not an obstacle to success for the person with a disability or for the people who support and care for them. It never occurred to me – even with the extreme challenges of raising my daughter – that there were restrictions on what I could do or achieve.

I have always loved learning about the relationship between mindset and personal development, which, in turn, led me to both start my own business and do formal study in that area. I now have a Diploma in Social Science and have taught human development for early education at Chisholm Institute of Technical and Further Education (TAFE). I also worked as a director of a local government childcare centre for a decade, and I am trained in Neuro Linguistic Programming (NLP) and was mentored for 18 months by Marianne Williamson during 2021 and 2022. Marianne is a four-time bestselling US author who was considered Oprah Winfrey's spiritual adviser, and campaigned to be the Democrat nominee in the 2020 US presidential election.

Because I love the study of mindset, I've always wanted to share what I have learnt with anyone who would listen. So, I started a business through which I offered mindset workshops and coached people about how the thoughts that we have and the things that we believe can affect our lives and our creativity.

Although I was coaching and running my business, I continued to study mindset. I was also implementing what I learnt into my family life. Miracles began to happen. Yes, I did just say 'miracles' because it felt that way. It is incredible how life can change for the better just by shifting your perspective on things and taking responsibility for your own beliefs and life rather than blaming others or feeling sorry for yourself.

As my business grew, I added women's business networking to what I offered. This journey lasted nearly two decades – all while I was raising a child with a disability. I had nearly 8,000 people attend my events; a social media following of over 12 thousand people, and at one point, I was coordinating 18 events a month, with leaders of each chapter of my network heading up their respective events. I even launched a system of national awards for women's businesses.

The challenge of prioritising my husband, raising our children – particularly one with a disability – and growing a business was, at times, overwhelming. Why did I continue? Because my business was my self-care! Running my business was for ME, and it gave me great joy.

Yes, it was challenging, but the study of mindset and its influence helped me with my relationships and my mental health. For example, there were times when I'd be ready to go to an event where people had booked and paid and were waiting to hear me speak or run the event, only to have the SRP walk out the door because my daughter was throwing a tantrum. I'd have to stop – knowing I would be late to my event – calm her down, sort out her problem, take care of anything else she needed and then pull myself together and go off to work as if nothing had happened.

One day I was talking to my husband about this scenario, and I said to him, 'If only those people who were at these meetings knew what I had just been through,' and again, with his great wisdom and sense of humour, he'd reply, 'Yes, but what about if only you knew what was going on in *their* lives before they got to your meetings.' In that moment, he put everything into perspective; that we all have our challenges.

During those years, a number of opportunities that were totally unexpected came up, including opportunities to join steering and advisory committees. As a result of joining these committees, I was able to advise on funds needed for children with disabilities.

The first committee I was involved with managed to get $5 million in funding, which went towards local schools to help them provide out-of-school programs for children with disabilities. At the time, these programs existed only for children in mainstream schools, despite being a much-needed resource for families with children with disabilities. Eventually, another opportunity came up where I was part of an advisory committee (as I don't want to get political, I won't mention names), but we were able to get $64 million allocated to create various organisations and services for children with disabilities.

I continued that inner journey of looking at all the possibilities, while taking responsibility for the situation and never blaming anybody else, nor having any expectation that the government or anyone else should be responsible for me and my daughter. And, as I continued that positive outlook, many things began to change.

The biggest positive change that has impacted our lives as a family is the introduction of the NDIS. Our daughter was nearly 15 at the time. As a result of the combination of the introduction of the NDIS and the impact COVID-19 lockdowns had on my business, I have pivoted my business from organising women's networking events to offering a service as a support coordinator in disabilities, and mindset coaching.

Great wisdom comes from life experience. I am able to work with people who have a family member with a disability to help them change their lives and experience positive outcomes. And it amazes me what and how much is possible.

My knowing and support of my clients and the positive results it yields comes from two decades of my own struggle, my own learning, and implementing what I learnt and then seeing the results in my own family life. I love what I do now! I love helping people with a disability and people who have a family member with a disability, as they navigate their personal outer and inner journeys.

# The Gift Of Learning, From Son to Mum

## Monique Peters

I once dreamed of being a teacher. Ironically, it was my son who taught me how to learn.

Listening to him talk these days is like hearing music to me. Lincoln, now 21, loves to talk about a wide range of topics; politics, philosophy, psychology and movies. It's a joy to hear him predict, analyse and test his theories on me. As a bonus for me, he adds depth with his growing knowledge of history. Hearing him speak, you'd never know how difficult it was for him to learn in a classroom.

If learning was difficult for you, how can you help other people understand what it's like for you? How would you articulate the frustration, when being eloquent eludes you?

When he was at school, his intelligence was masked by a learning challenge that wasn't easy to identify. He was in a gap, between the neuro-typical and those that had been diagnosed with a disability. At first, his challenges were subtle, and his teachers felt he needed more prompting. But as the learning became harder, the difference between him and his cohort became wider.

**Passing hearing tests, but unable to listen**

Without a diagnosis, teachers expected he could do better. Their comments were usually along the lines of, 'He could try harder.' Lincoln's peers also expected he could follow what they were saying and were frustrated when he couldn't. When he asked them to repeat something he didn't understand, they couldn't hide their frustration.

His grief was all caused by Auditory Processing Disorder, or APD. It's not a hearing or volume problem, so people who get their hearing tested will often pass, as he did, twice. APD is a problem with the way the brain processes the sound it hears. And as speech is so rapid, the APD brain can't catch all the little sounds that make up the words when we speak.

For many years I struggled to describe what it was like to have APD until the pandemic delivered the COVID mask comparison to me. As I laboured to understand many conversations with people wearing a mask, I was finally able to understand the difficulties Lincoln would have had in a noisy classroom, listening to the teacher. That explained how he seemed confused or even 'tuned out' altogether.

Experienced by as many as 1 in 10 students, the confusion created by APD is more common than many parents or teachers realise. It's about misunderstanding, and being misunderstood.

APD can be a diagnosis on its own, but it is also on a spectrum with dyslexia and being neurodiverse. Students with it are likely to have more challenges when learning to read. From birth, their brain may not have been able to make a clear map of the sounds of speech, or *phonemes,* as would be natural. To 'wire' or grow the neural connections for a good reading brain, it needs to hear and clearly distinguish lots of language in the first years of life. Without the ability to distinguish these sounds, the APD brain struggles to process and attach meaning.

**The price that's paid**

It wasn't so bad that Lincoln couldn't read at all, but working hard to put the words together, he'd also miss the point of the text. With a low comprehension, he couldn't remember what he had learned. I now know that APD made it harder for him to develop the skill of decoding, but back then, both the teachers and I could only say, 'You need to try harder.' Little wonder children with APD soon learn to avoid reading.

Learning to read can be a devastating time for students with APD. This is when they get left behind, as the class moves on to enjoy learning from what they read. When they avoid reading, their brain can't build the neural pathways to make reading fast and automatic. So, from Years 2 and 3, many children with APD stop believing they can learn. What's so sad is they don't know and can't tell you what is wrong. Instead, it may come out in their behaviour.

In Year 3, I was concerned enough to organise speech pathology. It unearthed a problem with his working memory, common in APD. At school, he wasn't finishing tasks, and 'incidents' increased. I was assured he would catch up, and that his progress was, 'normal for boys his age'. Unsatisfied, I downloaded maths and English worksheets for him to do, which of course, he didn't want to do.

By Year 6, I'd also put him through behavioural optometry and tutoring. Furthermore, he had endured some tough dietary protocols removing gluten, dairy and sugar. He resented all that but thankfully, now understands that a mother's worry can make her do 'tough' love, a little too tough at times.

I regret not making more fun for him back then. But all I could do was worry about the future.

At school, Lincoln couldn't find the words to say what he wanted, but now he can tell me exactly how he felt. His words sting. Guilt, sadness and anger wash over me as I am reminded of what I did. How I forced him to go to school, and didn't keep him at home where he felt safe. How he tried and tried so hard to learn as quickly as the others, and how cruel they could be. There's a strong, stabbing feeling in my heart as I write this. He reassures me with a forgiving smile now and again, a testament to his character. It's the rollercoaster of caring, I guess.

## Hope

Around the start of high school, his music teacher recommended a book called, *The Brain That Changes Itself* by Dr Norman Doidge. The book details recent developments in brain research, and tells true stories of hope. People who were born with severe learning challenges were accomplishing more than they were supposed to. Neuroscience research was revolutionising how we viewed the brain.

I was particularly spellbound by the chapter called *Redesigning The Brain,*[1] which talked about APD. Dr Michael Merzenich and his team of neuroscientists, had created an evidence-based online program. It could exercise, improve and strengthen the brain for the processing of language and learning.

It was also an odd, surreal feeling to read about Lincoln's challenges in a book.

Lincoln commenced the online program, and after three months, there was a significant improvement. Lincoln expressed himself more naturally, and he remembered more of what he was asked to do. About to start high school, this was a welcome relief. I relaxed and started to believe it was all going to work out after all.

His bullies didn't feel the same way. They couldn't let it go, or be kind in any way. They continued to be cruel. From stress, he developed severe reflux in Year 8, and wasn't able to digest large chunks of food. On doctor's orders, he didn't go to school for another term and a half. This was a great relief for both of us.

Fortunately, I found work supporting parents on the same program with a Sydney Speech Pathologist, and worked part-time at home. Lincoln and I were able to spend some time having fun, and enjoying longer conversations without the demands of school. As he relaxed, I'd get a glimpse of his true, inquiring nature. It helped me breathe, relax a little, and keep going.

---

[1] Doidge, Norman. 2018. The Brain That Changes Itself. Brunswick, Victoria: Scribe Publications, p45-92

I developed a keen interest in neuroscience at this point, so I undertook a lot of research and training. I was supporting and motivating parents and was amazed to see the students become more confident. I also saw improved literacy rates in schools, and how speech pathologists were using it to get better results for their clients. I was so inspired; I could not stop talking about it.

**Next level**

Then a coach encouraged me to start my own business. Could I really do something that courageous?

Thinking back over Lincoln's years at school, and how many children are in a similar situation, pulled on my heart strings. I thought of the students I'd supported over the last few years. They had all experienced what my family had to one degree or another.

I considered how many adults had come through the education system without being able to read. Not university level, but well enough to be able to get a good job or read a contract before they sign it. To many, knowing they were catching the right train or bus would make their life a lot better. How many of them had APD?

My heart went out to all the people who weren't living up to their potential, who may be frustrated or angry, on benefits, who had made bad choices, or even ended up in custody simply because the education couldn't understand them.

Then I thought of that child, who would be sitting in Year 2 or 3 right about now, just as confused as Lincoln was. I felt a fire burn, and my mission crystallised.

I needed to increase awareness about APD and the role it plays in learning challenges. And I really wanted to get the news out about neuroscience and learning.

Knowing me well by then, the coach set me a challenge to start in July 2018, and with the support and encouragement of both Lincoln, and my husband, I began my mission.

Getting the business started was overwhelming, as I didn't have a clue how to run one. All the learning, unlearning and relearning I had to do was incredible. There was also that voice in the back of my mind that said, 'You shouldn't be doing this. You're not qualified in anything, and it's not like your son is a famous success. Go back into obscurity where you belong.'

I swear, if people spoke to us the way we speak to ourselves, we'd tell them to get lost.

**Growth mindset –a fundamental learning skill**

As it happened, the 'growth mindset' was a body of research I came across while trying to find ways to motivate students. Psychologist Carol Dweck [2] had noted that some children were naturally more open to learning than others. It led her to separate the mindset that was 'fixed' on natural ability and a good result, from the 'growth' mindset that focused on the process of skill development. For me, it became clear that mindset was an empowering, fundamental skill for learning. I mean, why bother learning if you don't believe you can?

---

[2] Dweck, Carol. 2017. *Mindset*, UK: Robinson (updated edition)

At a different school since the reflux, Lincoln's mindset continued to plague him, and he struggled to retain friendships. I dreamed of a time machine that would take us back. I'd find out about neuroscience and the growth mindset when he was in Year 2, not Year 6, to a time before he lost belief in himself.

Finishing school in Year 10, he went to work in a local restaurant and got his driver's licence. The need for his own autonomy got stronger, and I knew I had to let go. I knew how important it was, despite his challenges. I'm glad my faith gave me the strength to do it. Thankfully, the business was a good distraction.

By this stage, I understood the growth mindset, and it helped me with the discomfort of learning new skills - as the mother of an adult, and as a woman in business. When COVID hit, I felt as though I could adapt and survive anything.

**We're always learning**

But part of that wisdom was knowing when to reach out for help. Fortunately, I made use of the skilled coach who gave me the original challenge. With fresh ways of thinking, I built the coaching skills and discipline I needed to serve my clients well. He also gave me the permission I thought I needed to speak up about my mission.

As a learning coach, I now recognise the deep connection to my childhood dream of being a teacher. Being open to learning is refreshing, and it means that no matter my level of skill in anything, I have the ability to improve it. It's about as empowering as it gets.

The irony of my son being my greatest teacher is not lost on me either.

Lincoln is becoming a man I admire. In some ways, he is still recovering from school, but a love of learning has been ignited. He is investigating less conventional platforms for learning and has plans for his own business. He recently started working with me as a Field Rep, talking to people in the street about APD and how Brain Wise Learning can help. The irony is not lost on me. Here is my boy, who struggled so much with communication as a child, and is out there now, educating, teaching, and changing lives.

He taught me about the plight of struggling learners, and he inspired me to launch a mission. One I hope, will change the learning and life outcomes for many.

Lincoln taught me that anyone can learn. Even me.

# Twins and Autism – A Life Changing Journey

Jenny Nechvatal

Every carer's journey is different, and I have found that no day is the same and even hour to hour, it can change.

My journey began 18 years ago in March 2005 when our paediatrician said, 'Jenny, Tony, your boys are autistic.' It was a short statement that would change the future for our boys and our family. Our twin boys were two years and three months old, and the diagnosis included intellectual delay. Our boys were non-verbal, and, as they got older, incontinent.

Our ideas and dreams for their future took on a new focus and led us on a journey that has taught us many things, has been frustrating, made us laugh, cry, feel angry and given us opportunities and experiences that we would have never had without these two beautiful children in our life.

There was a time of readjustment as we dealt with the realities of the diagnosis. Tony had always wanted his boys to play football and cricket, but these types of dreams had to be put on hold and then put aside as Ryan and Zac didn't develop the skills needed to participate in either of these sports. When Ryan and Zac were in primary school, it was difficult to see other children their age playing cricket and football or even just riding their bikes around the neighbourhood. You would look at children the boys' age riding their bikes together in a group, doing fun things together, being independent and giving their parents a break, but this didn't happen in our lives. The reality has been 24/7 care. Despite this, we have happy children and have built a life that meets our needs. We have learnt to be flexible, although sticking to a routine is essential with children on the spectrum.

The support workers, therapists and other organisations who have supported us over the years gave us access to some incredibly knowledgeable, caring, and talented people who have accepted our children for who they are. This included recognising their sister and her important role in our family, whilst helping us to accept and deal with the reality of life with children with a disability.

Knowing that there are people like this in our community makes you feel very grateful. We are thankful every day that there are people like this available to support us. When surrounded by such a great team, you can't see the world in a negative way when there are so many positive people impacting your life.

I had returned to full-time work as a Director at an Early Childhood service eight months before Ryan and Zac's diagnosis so my husband Tony could be a stay-at-home Dad. This gave him the opportunity to spend time with our daughter before she started kindergarten in 2005.

Working at an early childhood service meant the management committee consisted of parents who understood my need to attend therapy appointments with my boys. Each week we attended the early intervention service playgroup during term time and other appointments that arose. All the roles I have taken on within the early childhood sector gave me the flexibility to attend the numerous therapy appointments and meetings that come with a disability diagnosis.

In 2005 I decided to complete the fourth year of my teaching degree. There were major curriculum changes coming to the early childhood sector, and I felt that to lead my team and guide them through these changes, I needed to be current and set an example of ongoing learning. This was despite the fact that being a carer is an ongoing learning process that the staff experienced through me.

I completed the study over four years by doing a subject each semester instead of two subjects a semester over two years. I juggled parenting, working, therapy appointments, personal commitments, and study. It was a difficult, tiring, but enjoyable process. I look back and am proud of what I achieved. I also loved giving my daughter a strong role model to follow, and I am now so proud of her achievements.

In my role as Director and with the support of Tony, I had the opportunity to attend the Aspiring Leaders Forum in 2013. This gave me the opportunity to step out of the wife, mother, and carer role to inspire myself within the early childhood space, engaging in professional dialogue and discussing new ideas and theories. I think it is important to have a focus outside of the disability space as it mentally recharges you and gives you another focus, sometimes also providing ideas and solutions because your mind has had a break from the ongoing pressure of disability.

Engaging in other projects or activities means you aren't as focused on your world, so you notice that other people have challenges, not just you. There are times when we have been quite grateful that while our experience is challenging, we acknowledge that it could have been worse. We saw others that have more challenging lives, and we are grateful for the good in our lives.

Attending the forum led to presenting at the 2014 Early Childhood Conference in Melbourne; participants presented the individual research projects they had completed as a requirement of attending the forum. This was a whole new experience for me and a privilege to be able to present at a highly regarded conference in the early childhood sector.

In my director role, the educators that I worked with learnt from my personal experience and the way that I dealt with the families. This gave them confidence to build relationships with the families that had a child with a disability at the service, supporting the child and their family's inclusion at the service.

I recently returned to this service to ask for input on a book I am writing to support educators in understanding how they can better support families while creating an inclusive service. A benefit of having children with a disability, is that it gives you a totally different perspective that you can share with others.

Advocating for your children and within the disability space becomes constant as your children grow; every stage of development requires new supports, and new ideas to be implemented. This develops new skills and supports you to think outside the box. For me, this also flowed into my work in the early childhood field. There have been many positives from my boys' diagnosis that supported my role as Director or Teacher at an early childhood centre or teacher and Head of Department at TAFE.

As the Director of a service, I was able to help other families with children with a disability to feel comfortable when their child was at the service. I connected them with other disability services, provided practical ideas and, most importantly, could be a listening ear as someone 'who got it'. For these parents, it was so important to feel that they were heard and the challenges they faced were acknowledged. Sharing my personal experience with colleagues at TAFE allowed them to give another perspective on their teaching. The students I taught gained a new perspective and the opportunity to work more inclusively with children with a disability.

The National Disability Insurance Scheme (NDIS) has brought many positive changes to our family. We have choice and control over the services that our children access instead of receiving minimal services or spending hours advocating for additional services that we need to access therapies or respite for the wellbeing of Ryan and Zac and our family.

The opportunity to start my own business, Innovate Support Coordination, has arisen from the introduction of the NDIS. I understood the frustration families experience not getting the services they needed as they didn't understand the NDIS. Knowing from my roles in the Early Childhood sector that some families don't have the skills to advocate for themselves or their children, led me to set up my business so I can advocate for NDIS participants. My business also meets my family's needs as our boys move into adulthood.

When our daughter was in Yr 12, I reduced my full-time workload to three days a week, so I could spend time with her before she left for university. It is a difficult struggle to meet the needs of the sibling who doesn't have a disability. This is something we juggled over the years and sometimes felt we had failed at, but looking at the amazing person she is now, we know that we did a good job. She is a fully qualified exercise physiologist who will be working with NDIS participants. Her lived experience will be of enormous benefit to her employer and her clients. To support herself at Uni, she set up her own business as a support worker for NDIS participants. Her clients and their families loved her, and we are so proud of what she has already achieved at the age of 23.

There are some hard parts to deal with when you receive a disability diagnosis, and these challenges changed as our children grew. When our boys were younger and had meltdowns in public at ages three–four, people would look at you as though you were a bad parent. As they got older, people looked at you with pity, puzzlement or relief that it wasn't their child who behaved that way which did make being in public a little bit easier in some ways and brought us together as a unit in parenting our children.

A very challenging stage of our boys' disability was the aggressive behaviour they demonstrated as they moved into their teenage years. Luckily, they went through these stages at different times, otherwise I don't know how we would have coped. The aggression came in the form of biting, scratching, pinching, choking and, in one incident, a broken wrist for me as I fell over during a meltdown.

Our lack of knowledge of how to deal with this made it very hard. Ryan went from being a very happy and affectionate boy to one who could have outbursts at any time. His behaviour began prior to the NDIS, so trying to find professionals to help was difficult. We tried to find any support that we could. When Zac entered the same stage, we had the support of the NDIS, and more services and therapists or professionals available to support us.

A lack of awareness and understanding from the general community, which is understandable, made this an isolating time for our family. Family members and friends were understanding but, due to the behaviour of our boys, could offer little practical support. To help other families in the situation and to inform the general community about the reality of this aspect of Autism for some people on the Autism Spectrum, I am sharing something that is hard to talk about. It is embarrassing to say that your children have hurt you and to go out into public with bite marks or bruises on you that are visible.

This lived experience benefits the families I have worked with and some of my current clients. It is a relief for them to be able to talk to someone who understands and has had a similar experience, as no two experiences are the same.

A benefit from living through this experience is that I am less judgemental. I try to think of what others may be experiencing in their life before I judge their words or actions; this can even be with a cashier at the shops who seems abrupt. I stop and think that they may be experiencing a difficult time.

Living through unique and sometimes difficult experiences, you are prepared to listen to people and understand their individual experiences. I am more tolerant, and I think about what someone's story may be. The skill of looking at the full picture and considering how other people may have things that they are dealing with allows you to move through the day without letting small meaningless things annoy you. You have a much more open view of the world. Small incidental things no longer matter, your priorities take on a different order, and you add a richness and freedom to life when you don't worry about external input. You become stronger internally, which helps you to grow and develop and benefits your children as well.

Ryan and Zac are non-verbal, and this led to a whole new set of skills being learnt and developed by us so we could communicate with them.

When Kate was a baby, we said, 'We can't wait till she can talk, so we know what she wants.' Of course, like any parent, you sometimes regret when they start talking because then they never stop! However, at least you know what they want. With the boys, this never happened. So at 20 years of age, we are still sometimes guessing what they want, need or want to say. We are experts at reading facial gestures, using visuals, sign language or reading a situation to know what they want.

An example of this is I gave Zac his melatonin gummies the other night when he was in bed. Five minutes later, he came and took me by the hand, walked to his room, and stood by his bed. I checked that he hadn't wet the bed, there wasn't a spider or insect in the bed, and that his pillows were ok. I couldn't understand what he was trying to tell me. I was saying to him, 'Zac what's wrong?', knowing that he couldn't reply, but you still ask.

It suddenly clicked that I had given him his melatonin gummies five minutes earlier, and he was now directing his gaze towards the floor, so maybe he had dropped a melatonin gummy and yes, under the bed was one of his melatonin gummies. I picked it up and gave it to him. He popped it in his mouth and happily got back into bed. You become very close to your children to be able to read their needs and wants in this way. It also means you are versatile in many aspects of communication, which builds communication skills that can be used in professional and personal relationships.

Not only are we super communicators, we have learnt lots of other skills. For children and adults on the Autism Spectrum, keeping regulated and calm is essential. Techniques and strategies that work and continue to work are hard to find. What works one day may not work another day which is significant as it affects their ability to learn, cope with every day and engage in everyday life. Learning how to deal with this, liaising with therapists for ideas and other parents, or good old google brings about learning opportunities, and leads to creativity and problem-solving skills that you use in daily life.

Around the age of 13, Zac didn't want people in his home. He would become very distressed if friends came to the house, so our social life shrank dramatically, and we had to negotiate new ways of catching up with friends and family to maintain relationships. We are grateful that friends and family were flexible and would meet us out of our home at times that suited us. We also appreciate social media, which helps us to stay connected and reduces the feeling of isolation.

A diagnosis of disability totally changes how you think your life is going to be. There are a lot of adjustments, a lot of questions -why my child, why my family, why me? People would ask, 'How do you do it?' My response was, 'Well, they are my children. Why wouldn't I give them the best of care.' Or it would be, 'You do what you have to do.' Sometimes this would be said with pride and other times with sadness as it was hard, and there were days when you wished your child didn't have a disability.

Besides, why wouldn't you do it? You don't abandon your children just because they are not perfect. I feel privileged to have three children who are unique individuals, two of whom have grown into young men with their own strengths, interests, likes and dislikes who happen to have a disability.

Parenting children with a disability makes you so much more grateful, and you don't take things for granted like other parents sometimes do. You know that you have a richness to life that others don't. It has been a journey of small steps, each step can take longer than expected, and you will have progress then go back again. A tiny result can bring about joy and happiness and a sense of achievement for yourself and your child.

We have had many precious moments that are hard fought for that no one can understand until you have been through this. This gives you the hope to keep going, to start to realign your dreams of the future, and you begin to slowly see a shadowy glimpse of a brighter future.

Then you are living a life that is full, and busy, and you wouldn't have it any other way because if you changed your children, then they wouldn't be the unique and amazing human beings that they are. Their strengths, quirks, and personality traits wouldn't exist, and they are perfect just as they are.

# We Were Entrusted With A Child, Not A Syndrome: Justin

Alessandra Pelletier

My name is Alessandra Pelletier. My husband Jeffrey and I have eleven kids, and we make our home in Germany. My sister Irina, who lives in Australia with her family, encouraged me to write about my experience as a mom to a very special child, Justin.

Having kids is always an adventure - nobody knows what is behind the next bend. Every child brings his or her own unique personality traits into the family.

And Justin is no different. He is our 9th child. Our eldest son was 19 years and our youngest child was four years old, when Justin was born.

After a healthy pregnancy, Justin was born on 8th April 2005 - five weeks premature. As I had had premature babies before, that didn´t necessarily catch us by surprise. What did come as a complete surprise was what the doctor told us in the delivery room; that our child might have Down-Syndrome.

My husband and I were startled, to say the least. The diagnosis was confirmed shortly after Justin´s birth, and after just a few minutes in my arms, he was transported to a different hospital. As kids with Down-Syndrome often have heart defects, he was transported to a cardiological hospital that was two hours away.

After the delivery, I was wheeled into a hospital room. As I was laying there all by myself, I was trying to cope with the new situation. Jeff had gone back home to tend to the other kids. All kinds of thoughts were going through my mind. I was utterly confused, but as a devout Christian, I knew that God doesn´t make any mistakes and that Justin was part of a good plan for our family. And as I opened up my Bible, I read the following consoling verse: 'And we know that God causes all things to work together for good to those who love God, to those who are called according to his purpose.' (Rom.8:28). I was launched into this new adventure with this verse. It gave me the sure footing that I needed.

I still remember the many questions I had: Would I be able to nurse him? Would I be able to see him soon? Would I be able to be a good mother to this special child? Will he be able to walk and talk? So many questions, so many uncertainties.

This is what I wrote in my diary on the day following his birth: *At times I feel panicky about the diagnosis. Our friends have shown compassion and surprise. I want to learn to stand up to the decisions that we have made. Did God make a mistake? No, certainly not. He has everything under control. He will give me the strength that I need. He wants me to trust him. Justin needs me as his mommy. Just like any other child, he needs my unconditional love and support. I want to support him in his strength and in his weaknesses. Yesterday I gave all my maternity clothes away. I don´t think we will be having any more children. My distress has its place in God´s plan for my life. I want to live my life to his glory. Lord, help me to be grateful at all times.*

I was released from the hospital after a few days. I was glad that I was physically able to travel to the hospital to see my baby boy. We were very grateful that he didn´t have a heart defect after all, and after a couple of days, he was transported to a hospital that was closer to our hometown. Unfortunately, he had to spend some time in the ICU, where neither his dad nor his siblings were able to go see him.

This is what I wrote in my diary on April 14th 2005: *I try to pump my milk, but I am still very confused and sad. I long to hold you in my arms. At last, we were able to introduce you to your brothers and sisters. We stood by your bedside and admired you. You looked so perfect. We do look forward to taking you home with us! You were laying on your belly, and you were sound asleep.*

17th April 2005: *2 days ago, you were able to be transported to a clinic nearby. We have permission to hold you in our arms (I rejoiced!), and yesterday I was able to nurse you for the very first time!*

23rd April 2005: *I am so confused. Everything seemed so clear beforehand, and now everything seems so different. I do thank God for Justin, but it isn't easy for me to accept him the way he is. I struggle a lot, feeling envious of other mothers who have full-term pregnancies and healthy babies. I struggle with the fact that we have a handicapped child. But then again, isn't every child a blessing from God?*

Justin had to stay in the hospital for two weeks. As he was given formula at the hospital, I had a hard time nursing at home - he simply slept too much and had gotten used to the bottle. But I was determined to nurse him, so I tried my best to make that happen - and I did! Oftentimes I had to wake him, and if he didn't want to nurse right away, I pumped my milk and gave it to him with a pipette. It was a strenuous time, but we were happy to have him with us. His development was slow. We waited nine weeks for his first smile.

9th June 2005: *Time passes by so quickly. I have trouble keeping my head above water... A lot of things are going through my mind. I still struggle with the fact that Justin has Down-Syndrome. I want to learn to love him and accept him the way he is. I envy moms who have big, healthy babies. Justin is only slowly gaining weight. I guess that is part of him having Down-Syndrome....*

16th June 2005: *God takes care of me. He loves me. I want to learn how to best handle the present situation. Justin is not gaining any weight. I try to feed him as much as possible, but I am exhausted. It's not just him, though. The other kids are a hand full as well: Neal vomited a day ago, Vincent had trouble at school, Ryan kicked the glass door to the patio so hard that it cracked, Alaina was very demanding, and Aileen had to be picked up from her class trip, only to be taken there again soon---there were so many trying situations.*

Justin was about four months old when we started going to physical therapy. I enjoyed going to physical therapy with him since the therapists were always very kind and encouraging.

I made it a point to try out the different therapies that were offered, but I only stayed with the ones that I thought were really necessary.

This is what I wrote in my diary as Justin was six and a half months old: *Each day is a gift from God. I can see things much clearer now. God gives me the strength for my tasks. Children are his gift. If I have inner strength, I am able to be a good mother to my children. That amazes me somehow. Alyssa (15) has a girlfriend whose mother gave birth to a baby boy a week ago. But the parents are crying continuously as the little boy was born with a cleft palate. When Alyssa got to talk to the parents, she told them about her brother having Down-Syndrome. And she said, 'Your baby boy might have a scar for the rest of his life, but he will be able to lead a normal life. Justin, on the other hand, will have impairments for the rest of his life.'* This was consoling to the parents as they were able to see their son's ailment as something temporary.

10th October 2005: *As I was strolling through the park yesterday, it suddenly dawned on me: Justin is like a four-leaf-clover. There are not as many four-leafed-clovers as there are three-leafed ones. I want to enjoy this special child. Justin is such a gentle person; he is precious.*

In December of that year, Justin had to be hospitalised for a case of pneumonia. He was hospitalised for eight days, but he had to return soon thereafter and had to spend his first Christmas at the hospital in the ICU. It was a sad time for all of us.

12th December 2005 (the day after Justin was released from the hospital): *Justin was able to come home yesterday. Those eight days were a strenuous time for all of us, but I could see God's hand in it. At the hospital, I encountered a couple from India. The lady had given birth to a beautiful, healthy baby girl. But the couple was devastated, as they already had five girls and had wished for a boy. They were so unhappy about this girl. Their unhappiness was due mostly to the values they had accepted as part of their culture. And I could see that it was somewhat similar to the situation I was experiencing. Wasn't the prevailing message in our culture the following: Handicapped children are a curse, not a blessing? But I now strongly believe that handicapped children are like little angels that come into our lives.*

When Justin was 14 months old, I was invited by my brother-in-law to pay my sister a surprise visit in Singapore on the occasion of her 40th birthday. Since I was still nursing Justin at that time and was his main caretaker, I travelled with him. But that trip didn't work out so well. Justin had a lot of trouble breathing on the aeroplane, and once we arrived in Singapore, he didn't want to eat anything. Much to my sister's dismay, I had to take an earlier flight back home. Justin recovered as soon as he was back in his familiar surroundings.

As Justin got older, we had a lot of fun with him. I don't think any other child made us laugh as much. He was really cute.

He was walking at 18 months and started talking when he was four years old. That's when he started preschool (Kindergarten in Germany). He attended the same preschool as his siblings. We had considered sending him to one for kids with special needs, but the lady in charge of the local preschool encouraged us to give it a try. Justin enjoyed going to this preschool, but he didn't have any friends of his own. He was well-liked by the other kids though, and the childcare workers were very supportive. They were a big help in getting him potty trained at age six.

His eating habits were quite peculiar. Ever since his hospital stay as a one-year-old, he didn't want to eat anything but jarred baby food. He never wanted to give our homemade food a try. But he loved the dry dog food that was in the dog's feeding bowl. Did I struggle to keep him away from the dog bowl! I was always concerned about his vitamin intake as he refused to eat fresh vegetables and didn't care for most fruits.

Justin started school at seven years old. It was a school for special needs in the neighbouring town. And it was at that school that they encouraged him to try new foods. And I remember how surprised we all were when Justin all of a sudden took a piece of meat onto his plate while we were eating dinner. We were happy to see that he had finally come around to try something new.

Justin was almost two years old when Samuel, his baby brother, was born. And two years later, his brother Joshua completed the Pelletier family. It was a big blessing for Justin to have two younger brothers. It didn't take his younger brothers long before they 'surpassed' him as far as mental development was concerned, but his younger brothers were his favourite playmates for quite some time.

As my husband Jeffrey made it a point to introduce the kids to a variety of sports, all of our kids have always been very active in sports, and Justin was no different. From early on in his life, we encouraged him to do all the activities that his siblings were doing. He learned to ride a bike when he was three years old. He loves to swim, enjoys riding his bike, and is very active in a local roller skating club. He has even won competitions!

As Jeff had taken him to horse-jumping tournaments in the area, Justin has always been very fond of horses, and he was able to take up horseback riding as well. Another favourite pastime is playing minigolf with his dad. But as far as competitive team sports were concerned, we discouraged him from participating.

At first, Justin wanted to join his younger brothers in playing soccer and basketball, but we didn't want him to continuously sit on the sideline.

My husband lovingly called our sons, 'The three stooges'. They were a handful when all three of them were young, and at times things got out of control.

As I was reading through my other diaries (2006-2010), I realised that Justin's name didn't occur much at all anymore. Justin was just another family member.

As I was going through pictures, diaries and scrapbooks, I can say that the past 17 years have been filled with many fun activities, travels and events. As Justin wasn't physically impaired, he participated in everything.

Did we have any outside help? My mother had our kids periodically sleep at her house. That was always a special treat for them and us as parents. And, one by one, all of the kids got to stay at her vacation home in Turkey. Last year it was Justin's turn to travel with his older sister Alaina.

Justin's older sister Anika (she was 13 when he was born) was a big help when he was small as she loved spending time with her little brother. For a couple of years, she was very supportive. She would even take little trips with him to different locations. Once she got married and had a family of her own, it was Alaina who took a special interest in her little brother. They love spending time together, and at the time of writing they are looking forward to attending an ABBA concert together. Justin is counting the days.

I never insisted that the older kids take care of the younger ones, it was always a voluntary act on the part of the sibling. As I was able to be a stay-at-home mum, I tried to be careful not to burden the older kids with the younger ones.

Justin is able to read and write, but it took me a while to realise that he wouldn't be able to pick up reading as quickly as his siblings. It wasn't until I was introduced to a special learning program that he made progress. Now Justin reads fluently and simply loves his books. He loves going to the library. His math skills, though, are at the level of a first-grader, and that poses somewhat of a problem. As he wishes for a horse, a house and has extensive vacation plans, it is hard to explain to him that his allowance won´t cover those expenses.

Justin will be graduating from school this summer, and he is looking forward to it. Ever since last summer, he has been working at a local horse farm, and we are hoping that he will find employment in that area. Justin loves horses and enjoys horseback riding, and doesn´t mind the work involved in keeping the stables clean.

Justin spends a lot of time in his room listening to music, crocheting, colouring, putting up marble tracks and reading. He also enjoys activities with his brothers and sisters and has a few friends that live in proximity.

The past 17 years have had their ups and downs - isn´t that the way it is with every child?

Justin loves life and looks forward to the future. We don´t know what the future will bring as far as marriage, job or recreation is concerned, but we will continue as before, one step at a time.

We were entrusted with a child - by God.

# Fostering Is For The Open Hearted

## Irina Castellano

**Fostering is not for the faint hearted. It is for the open hearted** (Author unknown)

This book has many heart-warming stories about caring for your own biological kids. These kids have been with you since birth.

I would like to share my story of caring for kids who, 'were not born under my heart, but in it'.

A lot has happened to these kids before they even come into our home. All had suffered from some kind of neglect as a bare minimum and had just been removed from everything they had ever known before they arrived at our place, and that in itself is traumatizing.

You are told not to accept candy from strangers, but here they move right in with you.

Sometimes you find out a bit about them beforehand, sometimes they disclose information to you, and sometimes, you cannot explain what triggers these kids, and they themselves, can't remember as the memory is one of the things that goes (being the underdeveloped part of the brain due to trauma), when these kids grow up to fend for themselves, or when they live in a fight, flight, freeze or fawn scenario all their lives.

Having lived in eight countries due to my dad's work as an engineer, has made me very attuned to vulnerable kids. I moved schools many times. Being the new kid on the block, made me tougher in so many ways.

At the age of 15 years, I read the book, *A Child Called It* by Dave Pelzer, which had a profound effect on me. It chronicles Dave's story about how he was brutally beaten and starved by his emotionally unstable, alcoholic mother.

That's when I decided to one day foster a child in need of a safe home, and maybe even adopt a child, while always expecting that I would have my own kids too.

From the age of twelve, I have babysat in the neighbourhood. I went to France to work as an au-pair girl/nanny for two years, that's how much I like being with kids.

After having worked in the hospitality and airline industry, I finally met my future husband.

In 2000, I married my partner, and I moved from Germany to Sydney to be with him. There I was surprised to see the many ads in the local papers about fostering, and after convincing hubby of the idea, we became authorized foster carers in 2001.

After a few short placements, my partner accepted a role in China, then Singapore, and we ended up fostering there too. In 2004 we heard about a little baby needing a home, and we had a quick, efficient, Singaporean-style adoption process.

In the meantime, we had done several cycles of IVF, which resulted in a miscarriage, a stillborn and then a biological son in 2006. When we returned to Sydney, we continued fostering, and one child was not able to be restored, so we adopted her as well.

We are the proud parents of three kids, and although we still foster, I would like to dedicate my time and life to finding more carers as each child deserves a safe, loving home, and we have children sitting in motel rooms due to the shortage of carers.

As a foster carer, you need the willingness to learn about trauma-informed care practices. You need to stick to the truth. I don't sugarcoat things, but I also never ever talk negatively about the birth family, and I keep it age appropriate.

Kids are being removed from homes all over Australia every single night, and we don't have enough foster homes available to provide them with a safe family setting.

Feeling safe is a fundamental need for a child to learn, explore and grow. By observing how the caregiver deals with challenges, a child makes sense of the world. Trusting, consistent, loving relationships teach a child to name and regulate their emotional outbursts. A child learns strategies on how to do things better next time around if it is shown a new way forward.

Most kids that come to us are either extremely quiet while observing the new rules/boundaries/family dynamics, and then they open up or they come highly charged, not knowing what to do with all their emotionally charged energy.

Dr. Daniel Siegel says, 'How we experience the world, relate to others, and find meaning in life depends on how we learn to regulate our emotions.'[3]

For me, there is no such thing as a 'perfect parent'. We all try our best, and sometimes our best is not good enough, but it is rather important to show kids how we move forward from a situation that could have been handled better. Show them how to say 'sorry' and actually mean it. Teach them forgiveness and how to 'start fresh'. Help them heal by them knowing that you love them unconditionally, but you do not accept their behaviour necessarily.

As a foster carer, I aim to look past the behaviour and try to see it from the child's perspective. It is not easy (parenting, in general, is not easy), but trying to learn if there is a pattern, a particular trigger when a child does what it does, is a big part of working out where the behaviour comes from. When a child is attention seeking, then the child needs attention; there is an underlying reason for him or her to play up. Negative attention is often better than no attention.

Positive relationships are what a child needs, someone reliable, always there, no matter what. What happened in their past does not have to define their future. The brain can heal from trauma, but it takes consistency and time, often months, years or even a lifetime.

It is important to have a strong support network with like-minded foster carers around you, just like other carers in this book have highlighted the importance of being with

---

[3] Siegel, D. *The Developing Mind: How Relationships and the Brain Interact to Shape Who We Are* The Guilford Press, New York (1999) (p 245)

people who 'get it' as they have lived through something similar as well.

To open your home to a kid from a stranger takes a certain type of person. Foster carers can provide any of the four available types of care:

***Respite care*** – means that you get a beginning and end date to support the foster kids of another foster carer while they need to go somewhere, for example, into hospital for a procedure or for them to get a break to reconnect as a couple or to regroup with their biological kids because of the foster children's more complex needs, or for them simply to recharge their batteries.

***Restoration care*** – means that a child may remain in your care for up to two years, and the aim is to restore the kids to their birth parents or someone within the extended family/friends, to hopefully someone who already has a connection with this child.

***Permanent care*** – means that the child is unlikely to return to the birth family, and therefore remains in your care (as a ward of the state) till the age of eighteen years (and even longer, hopefully!).

***Emergency care*** – means that as a carer, you are on a 24-hour readiness list to be called anytime (mostly at night) to take on a child. You give your availability to your caseworker, who will inform the after-hours team.

We have provided all types of care over the years.

When a child arrives in the middle of the night, they might be carried in asleep as they have finally found a moment to relax, usually from complete exhaustion on the car ride to you. I would never wake them and just put them to bed as is, making sure there is a mattress protector as I don't know when they last ate, drank, or went to the bathroom. I'll put a snack next to the bed and a secure water bottle just in case they wake up.

If they are awake, they normally are fascinated with the dog and spend time with our Golden Retriever. Animals can help kids settle easily, and when a child is kind to an animal, it shows feelings and empathy, which is a great start.

There have been many amazing memories that fostering has created; we experienced many different challenges, and I couldn't have done it if my husband and kids had not come on this journey with me.

Our kids have shown these kids how to be happy children; they have held them, played with them, taught them to do a flip on the trampoline or how to take turns in games, and shown them patience and love.

It has also taught our kids compassion and empathy for kids who have a tough start in life, and they looked out for kids on the playground who were vulnerable.

To keep the hierarchy within a family, the foster kid is normally two years younger than your biological kids. All our kids have learned how to redirect behavioural issues and emotional outbursts with kids from all cultures and backgrounds. They have learned about the consequences of a one-night stand or what effects drugs can have on a baby in the womb.

They have seen me administer drugs to babies to wean them off drugs. Watching a baby going through withdrawal symptoms or seeing a child hurt when they can't see a parent in jail, are ways for my kids to understand certain aspects of life lessons they would take years to acquire.

We had kids who could not sit still to read a book, who would sit one second and then run around while I kept reading. Each day I would try, and each day they would come back more often, and sit another second longer until, eventually, they would sit through a whole book. Then they would sit closer and closer each day until they would want to sit on my lap and ask me to read the book, 'One more time'.

Those are the precious moments.

Or when a child does not want to be touched, and it is a struggle to hold hands to cross a road, until one day they cross the road and won't let go of your hand.

Before the first night at our place, I would ask if a child wanted a light on inside or outside of the room; or if they wanted the door open or closed. **One child answered, 'Door closed as the bad people come in at night'. This child had been sexually abused and did a full disclosure a few days later.**

It breaks your heart to hear this, and after a few weeks with you, it is gratifying when they love spending more time in their room as they learn that it is a safe place.

You can help them understand that it is NOT their fault that they are in care. It is so rewarding to see them take pride in their appearance, and in wanting to do better in school. They will insist on YOU tucking them in at night, and they will say, 'I love you' and really, really mean it.

They will disclose to you about their past because they have learned to trust someone. They will start to make plans for the future for the first time in their life. They will smile more because they feel safe. They will start to sleep without nightmares. They will stop hoarding food for the times when they might feel hungry again.

There are over 46,000 kids in out-of-home care in Australia, and we need 4,000 homes across Australia.

I am at a point in my life where I would like to help potential foster carers navigate the process of being authorized by an agency. There are so many agencies to choose from, and it can be overwhelming.

It has made me the person I am today, and I use this experience when I run the nationally accredited 'Shared Lives' Program for potential foster carers and the 'Open Adoption' workshops for potential adoptive parents.

If you have ever:

- Thought about becoming a carer.
- Wondered if you met the criteria as a foster carer.
- Tried falling pregnant, and it hasn't happened yet.
- Gone through unsuccessful IVF cycles.
- Wanted a sibling for your child.
- Been disheartened when an agency didn't call you back after an enquiry.
- Considered adoption/guardianship.
- Became an empty nester and miss having children in your home.
- Been interested in the A-Z of fostering.

Then contact me.

I jumped at the occasion to be in this book to create awareness of fostering and to find more safe homes. I don't want kids to go to motel rooms and wait for family homes to become available. There should be a long list of homes to choose from every single time a little one has to be taken away from everything they have ever known, as that is tough enough in itself.

My wish is to work closely with IVF clinics and to give clients hope who are unsuccessful with IVF. We have been through IVF, and I know exactly what it entails. I find it crazy to think that, on the one hand, we have many homes that want kids and many kids that need homes, and they are not being matched. With a bit of flexibility and patience, kids will eventually end up permanently, as many kids do get restored to birth families, but many do not. A judge presides over these cases; it is not up to us.

Once you foster, you learn a lot about the out-of-home-care system. The good and the bad, and you can make an informed decision if adoption is for you. All adoptions are open adoptions in Australia, which means that, most likely, you will have contact with the birth family, the frequency of which is determined and ordered by the court.

Fostering shows you how important contact visits are for a child to stay culturally connected, and it helps with their identity and to understand their medical history. These visits might be with birth parents, grandparents or any other important person in your foster child's life. Sometimes another sibling is added later, as many of these kids come from rather large sibling groups of eight to eleven kids.

Not that it is uncommon for me, as my sister Alessandra has eleven kids, and I invited her to write a chapter in this book as well. Her stories are incredible in so many ways. She has tremendous patience on a daily basis.

I'd like for readers to connect to find out if fostering fits your lifestyle, how your life may change and what you need to consider before starting. I am happy to guide you through the process of getting started and beyond.

I've been there, and I probably had the same doubts and concerns, but we did it, and I will always treasure each moment, challenging or not.

If anything in this chapter has resonated with you and if you would like to help a child in need, please contact me.

If you can help me spread the awareness through a podcast, TV station or an article in a magazine, contact me.

Post about it, contact with me on Linkedin, Facebook or Instagram (irinasyd).

On behalf of the kids in motel rooms, I appreciate your interest and time.

# Let Go Of Guilt And Embrace Love

## Graciela Ramon Michel

I don't know where to start; however, I am writing to you because I know I can help you.

I have been blessed with a beautiful family, Daniel my very supportive husband and my three children; Martin, who is 40 years old, nonverbal and severely autistic; Federico, 39, who is a brilliant person, father, husband, and professional, and Camille, who is 18 years old, and preparing to begin studying Marine Biology at Tasmania University at the end of January 2023. And now, as the most recent addition to the family, I have two granddaughters from Federico and Angie, Sofia and Martina.

Let me take you back to the beginning, to Martin's first year. I knew something wasn't right with him, but no doctor could tell me what it was.

Despite the wishes of my first husband, Martin's father, I began seeing neurologists, psychiatrists, and psychologists, but no one could give me an answer. I was seeing a therapist at the time, and I knew her colleague worked with children, so I begged my therapist to ask her if she would consider working with Martin and doing early stimulation tests despite her belief that he was too young. After much deliberation and discussion, I eventually got what I wanted for my son.

Martin was 18 months old at the time, and his actions were unusual for a child his age. I started looking for other options and reading as many books as possible because I knew something wasn't right. He was becoming more disconnected, avoiding eye contact, not responding to his name, making repetitive movements (flapping his hands and rocking his body), not responding to simple commands, and was hyperactive, to name some of the things I noticed.

My life with my morphine-addicted husband was becoming increasingly difficult to bear, so I decided to divorce him. Martin was only two and a half years old, and Federico was only 13 months old.

Suddenly, I was alone with two very young children, each with a very different mental state. Federico was growing normally. He was such a good little boy, with wide open eyes most of the time, when it came to his brother's behaviour.

My family and friends were unable to support us because everything was too unfamiliar and difficult for them. Little was known about autism back then, or at least not from where I came from, which is a small town in the North of Argentina. Nothing stopped me. I continued visiting doctors all over Argentina searching for an explanation for my son's behaviour.

When Martin was four, I had returned to Buenos Aires, Argentina's capital, for the fourth or fifth time in search of an answer. This time, to a doctor who was a neurologist and psychiatrist, and he confirmed the diagnosis, 'Your son is autistic.' I knew this by then, but it was extremely hard to hear it. Once I left the doctor's practice, I felt I was more autistic than my son. We crossed avenues without being aware of cars. At some point, we were almost run over. We walked and walked until night came, and I had no idea where I was, where I was going, or what to do; I was completely lost, my mind foggy, and my body aching.

The day after my son was officially diagnosed with autism, I flew back to Tucuman, where I was living at the time. I was very anxious because I had no idea what to do or where to go, which made me feel angry, lonely, tired, and overwhelmed. I also wondered, 'WHY ME? WHY HIM AND WHY US?'

My son's journey began there with various therapies, some of which were difficult to afford. I was divorced, a single mother, emotionally and financially supporting my children at the time.

My family and friends were drifting away from us because they were unable to help us and because Martin was showing very distressing behaviour. They felt confused and overwhelmed as well and didn't know how to react.

I am grateful that my father built a house for us to live in and provided food for us because my salary was insufficient to cover all of the house expenses as well as the treatments. My father's financial situation was a blessing for me. Martin's treatment took every penny I had saved up to that point, as well as every penny I was earning.

By the time Martin was five years old, I had decided that we needed to relocate to Buenos Aires (the country's capital) and consolidate all of his therapies under one roof. I had only been in the house my father had built for us for six months, so it was a difficult decision and choice, but I needed to try something different for my son's interest and for my own peace of mind, to be completely honest with you.

For two years, I lived like a zombie, never smiling, not knowing who I was, what I wanted, or even what I wanted to accomplish in my life, just doing what I had to do, a true GHOST in full survival mode. I worked 15-hour days and nights and was fortunate to live just a few blocks from the office. I took on the responsibility of taking my children to all of their activities, but I was completely disconnected from myself and not present for them.

I used to wake up with a horrible sensation in my stomach, lonely and hopeless, and I would constantly ask myself, 'Why me? Why him? Why us?' I couldn't see any way out, and my inner voice told me that I was only created to be punished indefinitely, that I was simply an unlucky person. By then, my level of thinking was so low that if I hadn't intervened and disrupted myself, I would have led my children down a dark rabbit hole.

And one day, I made the decision that I couldn't go on like this. It was a defining moment. So, I sought treatment, went to a counsellor, took meditation classes, went to the library and read books, and made the time, despite the fact that it was difficult to find an answer and direction so easily at the time.

I was learning how to navigate my emotions and the situations that surrounded them when I realised what it meant to be self-aware. I began recognising the times and circumstances that caused me anxiety or frustration and incrementally increased my confidence as I became more consciously aware of my emotions. I began to stop worrying about other people's thoughts and started to focus on what my sons needed. I began to develop resourceful strategies and learnt how to care for myself much better.

So, you're probably wondering. What exactly does it mean to take care of yourself resourcefully?

It means I found a way to look after myself and my family in a much more sustainable way. I learned about the idea of cause and effect, and I was able to stop living at effect (as a victim of my situation) and start living at cause (taking back my personal power to influence the situation in an empowered, positive way), accepting myself and my son's situation. It was an extremely powerful shift to learn how to take care emotionally of myself like this. As a result, I was more conscious and responsive, rather than reactive.

*"... the problematic situations in your life are not chance or haphazard. They are actually yours. They are specifically yours, designed specifically for you by a part of you that loves you more than anything else."(A.H. Almaas)*[4]

When Martin was eight years old, I had a life-changing experience that in reality, was a mind shift. I realised that Martin was a gift to me because he has taught me how to live a better life for myself. He has taught me how to become more compassionate to myself and others, and what empathy and love mean. Once I accepted life as it was, it took over, which means I was blessed to have him in my life. And I remain grateful to this day, despite the difficulties that his condition presents.

From there, another stage of our journey began. Even though his challenges were becoming more severe as he grew older, I was having more understanding of my son's

---

[4] Almaas, A.H., *Diamond Heart Book One – Elements of the Real in Man*, Shambhala Publications, USA 2000,

situation, and this realisation began to bring a little bit more peace into my life. Also, I had grown more dedicated to developing myself, and I had started to learn how to take care of my emotional needs.

I was reading a lot of books, including *You Can Heal Your Life* and *The Power Is Within You* by Louise Hay (who is my biggest mentor and the reason I am still with you and writing this chapter of the book). Other books I read as well are *Tapping Into The Power of Love* and *Many Lives and Many Masters* by Brian Weiss. I was beginning to appreciate life and looking for ways to improve as well as seeing obstacles as opportunities for growth.

With all this reading and self-education, though, do you think I was already in complete control of our lives and didn't need any additional help or support? Absolutely not. No, No, No, No! I was still stressed and anxious from time to time as I juggled work and study (to get promoted) against my children's demands and my own personal life as a single mother. Some days brought out the best in me and other days brought out the worst in me, and I used to project my needs and expectations onto my children. This was another major realisation and learning opportunity.

As I became more aware and conscious of my own triggers (through learning more about myself), my son became more aggressive, unpredictable, and hyperactive. He was far too difficult for any institution for children to handle. Most of the time, they would call me at work and ask me to go pick him up. It was a difficult time. I didn't know what to do, but due to the support I was getting, all of the books I was reading, and the meditation I was doing at the time, I was able to keep my mind positive.

Also, I have to tell you that Martin hardly ever slept at night, so he kept me awake for the majority of the night. Going to the toilet, climbing the fence naked, showering, and eating from the fridge were just a few of the things he did during the night.

Federico was fading into the background because he saw and felt how much I was struggling and didn't want to add another burden to my life; he was going bald from the stress of Martin's situation and my own overstretch as a single parent, and he had lost his hair completely at a young age.

My parents were saying, 'Please think about yourself and Federico, why don't you put Martin into a special care Institute.' To which I replied, 'Are you completely insane? I cannot send my son to such a facility; you have completely lost your mind.' Doctors began medicating him at the age of 11 because we couldn't handle him anywhere. It was the only option they gave me.

By that time, something that I was becoming more aware of was the time I was dedicating to Federico. We started to play golf together, and we brought Martin along with us, along with the lady who helped us to care for him. He used to get some peace and quiet on those golf courses. Those were happy times for me. I needed to do something for Federico as well, and I found something that was enjoyable for all of us in some way. Martin, however, stamped his own individuality in these episodes, including driving off with a golf cart on his own. He was 190cm tall with the strength of King Kong by the age of 14.

It was time for me, however, to face a longer-term consideration of how we lived; I had to do something about it and take action. He was having meltdowns on the street, pulling my hair, slamming me to the ground, and biting me, to name a few of his behaviours. The situation was spiralling out of control, and I couldn't take it any longer, so I began looking for places where he could be cared for at least a couple of days per week, allowing me to be more involved in Federico's life.

It was a long and exhausting search. It wasn't easy; as every place I went was inappropriate for him. I didn't want to find a place for him out of guilt.

Our lives had become a whirlwind by that point, so one day, I decided to choose one of the places I had visited in the previous months. Believe me, it felt like my life had been turned upside down once more. I'm not sure how I did it. For the first year, they would call me every night to put him to sleep because they couldn't handle it. His actions were upsetting the nurses, patients, and occupational therapists.

As a result of the accumulated stress and my body's exposure to extreme conditions, I developed pancreatitis and spent ten days in intensive care, with a better chance of dying than of living. The doctors couldn't find anything definitive that could have caused this because I didn't take any medications, drank alcohol relatively rarely, and didn't have any gallbladder stones. They explained that it was all due to the extreme stress I was under.

After spending time in the hospital, I began to find some peace in my life and began to enjoy every second of every day. Life with Federico was improving, and we occasionally played golf and tennis together. It was a memorable time for him, but he was approaching the age when being around his mother was no longer cool.

I was still feeling the pain of not having Martin living with us every time I used to go to visit him, and I also disliked my job, but I was making money, and that was what I needed. This time, however, I had another episode of pancreatitis, and my doctors gave me an ultimatum if I wanted to live longer, I needed to change my life, which really meant how I lived it. It meant putting myself first. After much deliberation, soul searching, and crying, I decided to quit my job and travel to Australia to visit a friend of mine who was living in Melbourne so I could continue my English studies. I planned to stay in Australia for 45 days, and this required me to organise my life, my home, and my children so that I could travel. My very existence depended on a concerted effort to change. This was everything; my sanity depended on it.

So, I resolved to begin living my life by choice rather than chance.

*"That part of you loves you so much that it doesn't want you to lose the chance. It will go to extreme measures to wake you up, it will make you suffer greatly if you don't listen. What else can it do? That is its purpose."(A.H. Almaas)*[5]

In the year 2000, I travelled to Australia and felt like a carefree teenager again, returning to school to study without the daily pressure of caring for my children. I was having fun with my friend and her husband, with whom I was staying, and exploring the city. It was wonderful to be able to go out to dinner without having to worry about my children. The sense of freedom, peace, and enjoyment was incredible. Only a few days after arriving in Australia, I met my future husband, Daniel, who was a good friend of the

---

[5] Almaas, A.H., *DiamondHeart Book One – Elements of the Real in Man*, Shambhala Publications,USA 2000,, p140

people I was staying with. This was an unexpected change for me!

To make a long story short, we went out and had a great time together in Australia while I was there, and by the time I had to leave, he had told me he wanted to get closer to me in a relationship. I immediately warned him that getting involved with a divorced woman with a lot of baggage and an autistic child might not be the best honeymoon or life. He was heartbroken, and I returned to Buenos Aires.

After I got back to Buenos Aires, Daniel came to see me in Argentina fifteen days later. Yes, you read that right; this insane Aussie was chasing me! My therapist questioned me and asked, 'What are you going to do now? Why don't you explore this, have some fun, and take a chance now that he's showing you a commitment signal?' 'WOW!!' I exclaimed.

So, I took the risk for myself; I went with an open heart, and after sixteen months of dating, we decided to marry in Buenos Aires. We lived between two countries for the next seven years, which was difficult for me. I kept my apartment in Buenos Aires for my son to live in so he would have something stable and familiar to live in, and we had to commute back and forth on visiting visas while I applied for Australian citizenship.

This was difficult because, for many years, I didn't feel completely at home in either country, and my life was divided between my children and my new life with my Australian husband. I have come to realise that my life and what I went through raising an autistic child was not a typical one, to say the least.

During these years, we had major issues with the institutions where my son Martin resided. Because of his behaviour, they were not coping well with him. Living in two different countries made this situation more difficult because I had to make frequent trips back to Argentina to help him with institutional problems. Martin has profound autism, he is strong and very tall, as I already mentioned, so there aren't many facilities that could take him in. It took many years to resolve, and it was extremely stressful, but I never lost hope because I found the strength and maintained a positive outlook and countenance with myself.

I persisted in my search for my son's suitable care institution. Finally, I found a place where he still is today, 16 years later, and where he is treated with so much love and care.

So many years of struggling to look after my son's condition didn't stop when I left to live in Australia, and looking back, it could have so easily defeated me. What kept me alive and positive with strength and connection was how I viewed challenges as opportunities. I chose to grow from them rather than surrender to the difficulties and the fear, and by doing this, I found greater happiness rather than perpetual disappointment.

This is the result of my rediscovering who I was, what I needed and wanted, and where I wanted to be. I found a passion for life and myself. My sense of authenticity, honesty, and integrity supported me and gave me the courage to take risks. I believe in myself, and I love myself and, above all, my children. I want them to see a happy mother who genuinely loves herself and her children. A mother who takes responsibility for her own actions, rather than hiding within herself or behind a slew of excuses. A mother that wants to continue evolving by being her own person, one who takes risks to succeed in life. I want to leave a meaningful legacy to my children based on my own authenticity.

MY BIGGEST PURPOSE IN LIFE IS TO **BE ME** WITHOUT EXCUSES AND TO HELP OTHERS NOT TO GO THROUGH WHAT I WENT THROUGH. TO CONNECT WITH THEIR TRUE ESSENCE AND TO LIVE THE LOVING LIFE THEY ALWAYS DESIRE BEYOND THEIR DAILY STRUGGLES.

**The best gift we can give to our children is our own healing!**

So now that I have defined my purpose and have written it down, as you can read from my own quote above, how have I put this into practice to help other parents? How do I connect with other parents simply to effectively make a difference based on what I have learnt?

By having combined my personal experience as a mother of a special needs son, as well as having established a successful coaching practise that guides and supports parents with a gentle and purposeful energy. To guide and support parents in moving beyond the worry and exhaustion to a empowered state of feeling guilt-free and energised, whilst thoughtfully building a rewarding life for parent/s to connect consciously with their child and develop strong bonds and celebrate the unique individuals they are.

Give yourself the love you deserve. You only have one life to live. You are worthy of making the best of it.

# Our Boy Who Changed Our Lives

Julie Fisher

In 2005, life was very busy for me and my family with two boys aged 8 and 5; Caleb was in grade 2 at school, and Blake was in 4-Year-Old Kinder.

Both boys were playing football, basketball and participating in Auskick, and I was helping with their sports as well as running the local Auskick Clinic. I was also enjoying helping at school and Kinder and was part of the Parents and Friends Committee.

I was working full-time in an administration role at an accounting firm both on their premises and for two days a week, working remotely so I could attend some of the activities at school with the boys.

I had always wanted another child, but we had decided not to go ahead because we were both getting older. I was 36 in 2005, and Mick, my husband, was 43. Earlier in that year, we thought I was pregnant, and I was thrilled, absolutely over the moon. When it turned out to be a false alarm, we were both disappointed, so we decided to go ahead and have another child.

I became pregnant very quickly and talked with my employer about taking the same amount of maternity leave as I had previously, and about the possibility of working remotely for three days. Planning is something I've always liked to do so I can have everything sorted in my head.

As the pregnancy went along, and I had my scans, there was an indication that my baby may have an issue, and I suspected Down syndrome. Nothing was said in the early days, but the actions and tests that were happening led me to believe this was what we would eventually discover.

The year before I became pregnant, I became friends with a lady named Tina who has a daughter with Down syndrome, and I used to ask her many questions like, 'When you received the diagnosis, how did you feel?'

I remember her telling me how devastating it was when they first heard those words and how everyone was initially extremely sad. I remember telling myself if that ever happened to me, I would want to find out before the baby was born so there would be no tears when they entered the world. Little did I know back then what was going to happen.

Following my scans, I had a gut instinct that my baby did have Down syndrome, and after discussing this with Mick, we decided to find out so that if this was the case, we could tell everyone before the baby was born.

That way, we could learn about what the baby would need, learn about Down syndrome, and go through the emotions we knew we would need to. We wanted to tell everyone so there would be no tears when the baby joined our family.

We received the diagnosis at the 15-week mark of the pregnancy, and there began the emotional rollercoaster ride. We also discovered we were having another boy and named him Darcy. We began telling everyone the news and got comments from some people that we weren't expecting. These comments shocked us, but we pushed our way through with support from family and friends and I started trying to map out what the future may look like.

Entering the world of disability was very scary because it was the unknown and was not the road we were expecting to travel.

Because of making friends with Tina two years before I became pregnant with Darcy, I was able to engage in a wonderful support group she was running with other mums while I was pregnant. She ran a fortnightly coffee/support group, and as soon as we received the diagnosis, I was able to join that group.

I remember walking in the first time and looking at all these mums with so much admiration. They were travelling on the road I was heading towards, and they were so supportive. I was able to connect well with them all, and ask them any questions I had. I was also able to see their children and watch how they interacted with them and each other.

The ages varied from babies to 7-year-olds, and I was able to learn about therapies, strategies at home and I was also able to hear about what they were all doing with schooling. This group was an enormous help to me.

My plan to tell everyone so that there were no tears at his birth, happened exactly how I envisaged. He came into the world like a rock star and has never experienced any sorrow. Even though there were still many questions and emotions, he was accepted into the world just like his brothers were, with happiness and excitement.

When he was born, I began hearing the words 'unpaid carer' in reference to me, and I really struggled with that title. It wasn't on my radar at all. I didn't even realise there was such a title until I entered the world of disability. I was his mum, but apparently, I was also his 'carer'.

During the early years with Darcy, I found it very difficult to relate myself to his 'carer'.

Even with the extra appointments with doctors, hospital visits and therapy sessions, I felt I was just doing what was needed for my son as his mum.

His general needs as a baby and young child were the same as his brothers for quite some time, so when my friends with children with disabilities told me I should register with Carers Victoria, get a Companion Card, and look for support for me as a carer, it just felt strange.

He did have a lot of extra appointments with doctors, specialists, and therapists, but what I provided for him at home as a baby with feeding, changing and playing, was no different to what I did for his brothers.

It wasn't until he was in the later years of primary school that I began to understand the title of 'carer'.

Even though at the same age, while in primary school, his brothers were still coming everywhere with me, and I was taking them to their sports training, parties and walking them to school just like I was with Darcy, his needs at home were very different to theirs at the same age.

When I think back now, when we were going through all the hospital visits when he became ill, as well as regular paediatrician appointments and therapy appointments, I was going on autopilot. Even all the extra things I was doing at home, I was doing these as his mum. I recognised what things were required for my boy and just made sure everything got done.

Enjoying times when he was at home with the family was very special because, especially when he was younger, we never knew when he may end up back in the hospital. We spent many months in and out of hospitals for the first 18 months of his life and then up to the age of 14, having regular six monthly checkups with the gastroenterologist, the PEG outreach team, dietetics, and the paediatric lung specialist.

As he grew and became stronger, the appointments became yearly, and we were eventually discharged from the lung specialist we had been seeing. I remember feeling a little sad when he discharged us. Don't get me wrong; I was pleased because it meant Darcy's lungs had healed, and he was doing well, but this man was a wealth of knowledge, not only in his specialised field, but with many other things. He was extremely kind and had an amazing bedside manner. He always spoke with kindness and compassion, and it was great to see him. He was always extremely supportive, and nothing was ever too hard.

Another reason was that I felt that he saved my son's life, and for that, I am forever grateful. I didn't want to let go of it, but I understood I needed to, so we could move on.

I continued to attend the support group. I was in awe of these women and thought they were amazing and very special, but now that Darcy is 17, I know they were being Mums and doing whatever they needed to do for their children. Like we all do.

Recently I was speaking with one of those Mums, and she recalled the first day I walked into the support group. She said they were all talking about me before I got there and were in awe of me because I knew Darcy had Down syndrome. She said they all thought I was very strong.

Once we received the diagnosis, and before Darcy was born, I had made the decision not to return to full-time work because I knew his appointments and therapy sessions would be during the day, and I wanted to be available to take him to all of those. So many things were changing very rapidly.

I had been working in the accounting field for 18 years and, with my other sons, had continued to work full-time once returning to work. With Caleb and Blake, I returned to work when they were three months old, but with Darcy, I didn't go back to work until he was 12 months old in a completely different field of work than I had known.

I was fortunate to be offered work in the hospitality industry by a friend, and I began by working one evening shift a week. Over time, this increased to three shifts a week, and I was able to be at home during the day for all the boys including being able to take Darcy to his appointments.

Working full-time wasn't an option for me when Darcy was born because of the extra appointments and therapies he needed. He also became quite unwell when he was three months old, and for a long time, we were in and out of hospital until it all became stable.

It was such a scary time, not knowing whether my little boy would survive. We discovered he had been aspirating his bottles with every feed, and probably from birth. He hadn't been putting on a lot of weight, and this was one of the reasons why. His little lungs were filled with fluid, and he had to be put on oxygen for a few months to help shift everything so he could breathe properly. Even that took some time to get right and was something new I had to learn to help my boy.

After many months, scans, x-rays, and other tests it was discovered that Darcy couldn't tolerate any thickness of fluid at all. Everything we tried to give him in the bottle, went into his lungs. The next step was for him to be put on a waiting list for a PEG (Percutaneous Endoscopic Gastrostomy). This is where they place a flexible feeding tube through the abdominal wall and into the stomach. It allows the feeds to go directly into his stomach, bypassing the need to swallow.

While we were determining the best thing for Darcy, we started him on solid food to see if he could tolerate that. Thankfully, he did tolerate the solid foods, and now, at 17 years old, he drinks orally and independently again. We spent two years teaching him, and because he could tolerate solids, he was able to keep the chew and swallow reflex. I am so thankful to all the specialists during this time for helping our boy.

With the PEG, this meant adding more regular appointments to our schedule. We had early intervention, speech therapy, occupational therapy, paediatric appointments, gastroenterology appointments, PEG Outreach team appointments and dietetics appointments.

Having the flexibility with my hospitality job allowed me to be able to make sure everything Darcy needed, was able to be provided. It was an extremely busy time with all these appointments during the day and then his brother's activities, but we made it happen and made it work.

Darcy is 17 years old now, and his brothers are 23 and 26. His brothers don't need me to get them out and about anymore or tend to any of their needs. They are still at home and have a great relationship with Darcy. It's beautiful to watch.

Darcy still needs me and will for quite some time to come. He needs assistance with meal preparation, all of his self-care needs and cannot go into the community unless he has someone with him.

We have some amazing supports set up for him, and he enjoys doing all his activities with support workers individually as well as in a group. This gives him a sense of independence because he doesn't have me or his dad with him all the time. He's creating some wonderful friendships with these groups, and we have the knowledge that he is being cared for.

There is also always lots of planning to be done with many things in Darcy's life. Every time something new comes along, it's a lot of paperwork as well as ensuring these new things will meet all his needs.

I am always thinking forward as much as I can so I can be aware of all his options as well as knowing about everything I need to do to make things happen as smoothly as possible such as his Disability Support Pension. I started gaining all the knowledge about this three years before the application process was to begin, so I knew exactly what I needed to do to make it as smooth as possible.

There are many things that Darcy needs help with and many things he may never be able to do on his own, but this young man has taught me so many lessons since he joined our family.

He introduced our family into a world we never expected, and we found ourselves among many others who were accepting and supportive. They are people who help when needed and raise each other up all the time. The community our boy introduced us to is amazing.

He showed us the world through his eyes, teaching us unconditional acceptance and inclusion. Seeing everyone for who they are and hearing their voices with no judgement whatsoever.

He has taught us to think outside the box, never give up, to have much more resilience than we thought we had and to advocate for him to ensure he is able to do anything he would like to do.

As his mum, he has been the inspiration for me to take a leap and do something I'd always dreamed of. He is the inspiration for my books, *The Unexpected Journey*, *The Magic of Inclusion* and *From the Heart of Mums*.

Because of Darcy, I found the passion deep inside of me to advocate and raise awareness not only for him, but for many others who live with disability. He has led me on a new, unexpected journey of assisting other families, becoming a radio host, and accomplishing another dream of doing a TedX Talk. My third book *From the Heart of Mums* was recently released in April this year. I have published many articles, worked with organisations in the disability sector and spoken publicly to continue raising awareness.

He introduced us to the world of disability, and even though it was a little scary at first, once we began meeting other families with children with Down syndrome, we could see that this new world was one full of acceptance and guidance.

The people we have met help each other and give amazing support. We are blessed to be part of this.

Darcy taught us about Down syndrome and the many different aspects of this. Just like the rest of us all over the world, everyone is different in so many ways. I wrote this about what Darcy taught us:

*He taught us to be patient.*

*He taught us to be advocates and stand up for his rights.*

*He taught us to think outside the box – there is always a way someone can participate no matter their ability.*

*With love, guidance and support anyone can participate and enjoy many things.*

*He taught us to embrace every opportunity that comes your way.*

*He taught us to enjoy every moment as though it's the first time you are experiencing it.*

*He taught us it's ok to need help.*

*He taught us everyone is different and the same no matter what – disability or no disability.*

*He taught us every single moment counts.*

*He taught us it's important to stand up for your rights.*

*He taught us to share our journey and teach others.*

*He shows us all the best unconditional love you could ever experience.*

*He shows us how blessed we are every day.*

*Yes, it can be hard, but…*

*We wouldn't change you for the world, but we will change the world for him.*

*Give People a Chance and Watch Them Shine.*

# Life Is Mainly Froth And Bubbles

Nicole Dunn

There is something special about the relationship with a grandparent. No matter what you do, you're never in trouble. The only time my Nanna ever yelled at me was when, as a two-year-old, I thought it would be a good idea to stick a pen in an electrical socket. Even then, all I got was a stern, 'Nicole'. The love is unconditional; at least, that's how it was with my Nanna.

Roma Dunn, my Nanna, was someone I always admired. She was ahead of her time yet always humble. Nanna raised two children, my father Andrew and aunty Karen and kept 'the home fires burning' when my grandfather was on dangerous overseas missions as a UN chemical weapons inspector. No matter what bump in the road, her outlook was always the same, 'There's no point worrying about it, dear.' Although I'm sure this outlook was tested after my grandfather passed away.

When I moved to London, Nanna visited, even coming to the pub with my friends to enjoy a few drinks of Pimms and Lemonade. When I returned home after the big adventure, but with little money, the door was already open for me to stay with her.

My brother and I occasionally spoke about the day when Nanna may need more help or, God forbid, couldn't drive as she was always so proud to be one of the last of her friends to still be driving. At the time, the concept of 'the day' seemed like a lifetime away or not even a possibility. I'll never forget the day it all changed. I was finishing a shift working in emergency, when my aunty phoned, panicked that Nanna had jaundice and was told by her doctor she should go to a hospital. 'Bring her here', I said nonchalantly. I'd just finished work, it's not like it was a big deal, and everything would be sorted in no time, or so I thought.

I was sitting in the emergency cubicle with my Nanna pretending everything was fine whilst trying to decipher the unusually quiet nursing handovers. The nursing handovers were almost like Morse Code. Knowing I was one of them, a health professional, I didn't have to wait much longer to crack the code, yet ironically, I wish I never knew.

The doctor, my colleague, called me over. I knew it was bad as he was in 'professional mode', clinical and matter-of-fact. 'We found something on the scan,' he said with a stony face. 'It is pancreatic cancer, and it has spread. It is terminal.' Each word pierced like a bullet. One year was the prognosis.

My world was shattered. I'd only ever mentally prepared for my Nanna to need a bit of help at home or not be driving, never this. How was this even possible? She was still so active. Nanna wasn't a sick person. Suddenly nothing was familiar, and nothing seemed right in this world.

Immediately I took on my own 'professional mode' and got to work. Within days I'd terminated a lease on my rental property and started the process of moving in with my Nanna, knowing she would need the extra help. Despite the terminal diagnosis, my Nanna's biggest worry was making sure moving in with her was something I wanted to do and that it wouldn't hold me back. I never thought twice about it. I did have two stipulations though; to get the internet and upgrade from the available single bed in my Nanna's home. The deal was done.

At the time I was caring for my Nanna, I was 32, and Nanna was 83 years old. I had no kids and had never looked after anyone. Taking care of a cat was the greatest responsibility in my life so far. My father had just moved to Darwin for work, and my aunty was already a carer looking after her husband, who had end-stage liver failure. Our family was small, and I was the eldest of four grandchildren. I was working full-time as an Emergency Department Care Coordinator and physiotherapist while balancing a new role as a live-in carer.

I only took two days off work after my Nanna's diagnosis, which in hindsight, was not enough. I returned to the same department, seeing patients in the same emergency cubicle where I was told my Nanna had one year to live. Work was a constant reminder of my Nanna's diagnosis, but at the same time, it was a welcome break from being a carer.

There was the constant guilt of not wanting to let down work colleagues if I took time off. At the same time, I didn't want to let down my Nanna if I wasn't there. It seemed like a no-win situation. I decided to reduce work to four days per week, which was a huge relief, and I was a more productive employee and carer by having a better balance.

With time I found a routine. Chemotherapy most weeks, arrange a blood test a couple of days prior to chemotherapy, doctor visits and specialist appointments. Knowing Nanna's health would decline, we arranged services through My Aged Care and a visit by an Occupational Therapist. The phone calls from service providers, which were always during business hours, seemed endless. On top of the new appointments, there was still all the regular life routines to contend with. Completing a tax return for someone who was starting to forget their finances was one of the most arduous challenges.

But at the end of a long day, we would sit and watch TV together. It may have been the only hour I wasn't running around making sure everything was prepared for the next day, and I cherished that time. We would watch our favourite TV shows, make jokes, and talk about our day. Our relationship was the closest it had ever been. I learnt to be humble, caring and how to get through adversity, skills that would serve me for a lifetime.

Despite my lack of experience as a carer, I was figuring it out, and I had the advantage of working in healthcare. As a health professional, I had the golden ticket. I had the inside knowledge that others often longed for. If only it was that simple.

When the hustle and bustle of moving in with Nanna and arranging appointments settled, I found myself in emotional turmoil. I was in a state of shock and grieving that someone I loved so much and who was so strong had pancreatic cancer, and their life was now on a timer. The pool of helplessness was so deep watching a loved one decline before your eyes, knowing there was nothing you could do to fix it or make it better.

Just the mention of my Nanna's name would send tears flowing. My friends were supportive but were on a different path in life -marriage and babies, and I didn't know anyone else my age caring for a family member. I spoke to a psychologist and was told I was experiencing an acute grief reaction. It felt good to know what it was, and I could stop beating myself up because 'I should be happy' or 'I should be grateful that my Nanna is still here'. I now understood that what I was feeling was valid. No healthcare training ever prepared me for the emotional roller-coaster of caring for a loved one.

I knew I needed an outlet which for me was always sport and exercise. I came home one evening with a pair of new football boots and told my Nanna the following day I was playing AFL with my cousins for a local team who needed a fill-in. I'd never played AFL before! One fill-in game turned into the rest of the season, and the season after that. Rain, hail or shine, Nanna was at every football game as our biggest supporter.

If the weather was poor or she was tired, she would sit in the car and honk the horn if we got a goal. All the girls in the team loved her, and she became the club's unofficial mascot. Nanna even used the football matches as an excuse to get out of the hospital early. During one hospital admission, she politely told a doctor, 'I couldn't possibly stay in hospital over the weekend, I've got three granddaughters who all play football together, and I watch their matches every week'. She must have been convincing as she didn't miss the next match.

It was often the simple interactions that become the most memorable. Nanna loved her family doctor, and she often commented on how he, 'was so lovely' and that he had 'really nice teeth.' I'd glance over at her when driving away from an appointment and ask, 'You've got a crush on your doctor, haven't you?' She'd chuckle and look back with a cheeky grin and say, 'Well, he is very nice,' before telling me the next shortcut I could take to get home.

When Nanna could no longer be at home and needed care in a nursing home, it was tough. Nanna declined quite quickly over a month. She fell over twice at home when I wasn't there and accidentally double-dosed on her medications. I came home from work one day to smell burnt food. Nanna reassured me she burnt toast, however I knew that wasn't the case. A year after my Nanna passed away, I found a burnt pot shoved in an outside cupboard. It was a decent effort to conceal the evidence.

One of the hardest conversations was to tell Nanna that no matter how much I wanted to care for her at home, I just couldn't anymore. The care she needed was beyond what I could provide, and unfortunately, with a mortgage to pay, I couldn't quit my job. I reminded Nanna of the promise I made her when I first moved in, 'If it was ever too much to care for you that I will let you know.' She understood and seemed accepting; it was such a relief.

A week later, Nanna forgot this entire conversation, so we sat down and had it again.

It was so quiet at home without her, and time passed slowly. The first month in the nursing home was challenging for my Nanna and my family alike. Nanna was more confused, and she made two stealth attempts at escaping. I arrived one morning to find Nanna reprimanding the staff and waving her finger in their face, something I'd never seen before. I asked what was wrong, and she told me 'I'm meant to be going home, but these people won't let me.'

She had clearly forgotten she was in her new home. I walked over and said, 'C'mon, let's go into your room and have a chat about it.' As I walked into Nanna's room, my jaw dropped when I discovered she had packed every item in her room. Clothes, towels, bed linen, food, toiletries and homewares were now in suitcases and garbage bags. Nanna even pulled all the photos off the wall and unplugged every appliance, even turning them off at the power point, clearly very energy conscious!

When I reminded Nanna she was home, her face was more shocked than mine, 'Oh, I've caused you a problem, haven't I, dear?' I reassured her it was nothing we couldn't fix and joked she deliberately packed everything up just to show me how to clean and fold things properly. The second escape attempt was on Christmas day, and we all burst out laughing when my aunty explained why they were late for Christmas lunch.

Nanna eventually settled at the nursing home, and we made the best of the situation. On Friday nights, we would pick up pizza from the local La Porchetta for 'Pizza Night', a tradition that continued from her time at home. My brother brought his dog Indy to visit Nanna at the nursing home, which she loved, and Indy even managed to have his own mat in Nanna's room hidden under her hospital bed. We arranged a bar fridge so she could continue to entertain her guests with food and drink.

After initial doubt, I realised I was still a carer. I was just supporting Nanna at a different place. We developed a new routine and got to know the staff and residents alike. On one visit, Nanna was hurrying off with a friend to the monthly residents and staff meeting. She promised she'd go even though she really didn't want to. I was also roped in and ended up in the front row with her. We both laughed like naughty schoolchildren, with the first order of complaint called out from one of the residents was, 'Not enough salt and pepper on the Friday fish.' 'That man is always difficult,' Nanna whispered.

Roma Dunn passed away in 2017.

Whilst you might not be able to make someone else better, you can always make a situation better. A smile, encouraging words, a timely joke or just talking about your day, these little things make a big difference. What starts out as a routine day can easily spark into a memory cherished forever. When the curtain has closed on the life of your loved one, as a carer, it's the moments you may have never expected that make you smile when the person is gone.

Being a carer gives you a certain power that no matter what crops up in life, you can deal with it. There are very few things harder than being a carer, and you never know what opportunities will come from it.

In 2015 I started my own business, 'Empower Aged Care Consulting,' which is still running today. Through my business, I act as an older persons' representative with My Aged Care to ensure they receive the home care services they need. It's rewarding meeting other carers and being able to help. Prior to being a carer, I had only worked in public health and never dreamed of starting a business.

In 2019, I spoke as a carer at the Royal Commission into Aged Care Quality and Safety to share my story, raise the profile of carers and hopefully see systemic change. I wore my Nanna's bracelet on the day as a reminder of her

At an event for carers week one year after my Nanna had passed away, I received a tap on the shoulder from a person I'd never met, who said, 'You're Roma Dunn's granddaughter, aren't you? You're just like her.' Turns out this person was a friend of my Nanna's and had seen some of the work I'd been involved with.

My biggest achievement will always be the care I provided to my Nanna in her last two years of life. The knowledge, love, care and life skills she taught me as a carer far outweighed what I ever gave her. To appreciate the little things and live in the moment is one of the greatest gifts one can receive.

For as long as I can remember, my Nanna had a magnet on her fridge containing a mantra she lived by extracted from the poem *Ye Weary Wayfarer* by Australian poet Adam Lindsay Gordon. It resonated with me as a carer, and I'd often read it when I walked through the kitchen.

> Life is mainly froth and bubbles
> But two things stand like stone
> Kindness in another's trouble
> And courage in your own.

# Of Course Our Son Brought Us Joy. Why Wouldn't He?

Lorraine Gaunt

My name is Lorraine, and I have been married to my beautiful husband, Adrian, for 34 years. We have three children, Christopher, 30, Daniel, 25 and Stephanie, 23.

When I was invited to write my story about being a carer, I thought for a long time about my experiences and what I wanted to share. It would be so easy to share negative experiences and the trials and tribulations of being a carer for a child who has significantly higher needs than others, but we all face challenges in our life. It is facing these challenges that mould us into the person we are. It is how you face the challenge and come out the other side that makes you a better person. My son has made me a better person, a better mum and our family, a better family. We are who we are because of our amazing son, and I would like to share with you, all that we have achieved with him. I want to share the amazing experiences that Christopher has brought to our family.

In 1992, I was a secondary maths and science teacher eagerly awaiting the birth of my first child. I wanted to do more study, but I was not sure which path to follow. In my teaching career to date, I had worked with students who struggled with mathematics, and I enjoyed it, but I also enjoyed helping and counselling students. I was considering if I should do further study in special education or in counselling. Then, my son was born. After a week, we found out that he had Down syndrome.

Like many people, I really didn't know very much about Down syndrome, and I was scared. I was scared that the life I had seen for myself, further study, further teaching, leadership roles, and many other things could not happen. I was fortunate to meet with another young mum who had a son with Down syndrome. I asked if I could go back to work, and if I could achieve all of the things I had thought about doing. Her advice to me was that if I had planned to go back to work or to go back to study, I should, and could do these things. My son was going to need more help, but so did lots of children.

I was scared as I did not know what to expect from my son. I did not know what he could achieve; I did not know what his future would hold. Interestingly, when my second son and my daughter were born, I also did not know what they could achieve. I also didn't know what their future would hold, so why was I so scared about this for my first son?

So, what did life look like for our family? Well, yes, there were tears, there were difficult times, and there were frustrating times (mostly frustration in dealing with bureaucrats!). But there were also so many causes for celebration. Christopher has brought all the joy to our family that any first son should bring.

We marvelled at his achievements and celebrated his milestones as he learnt to sit up, to crawl, when he grew his first tooth, learnt to walk, to run, to ride a bike, and even when he fell off his bike the very first time.

He went to little athletics and enjoyed competing with his peers. He was a founding member of the Jimboomba little athletics club, and at his final year presentation when he was 16, we were so proud to see him presented with the sportsmanship award, an award that his peers brought forward to the parent committee to honour everything that they had learnt from Christopher in his ten years at the club. His peers presented him with an award for his excellence and commitment to athletics, for always trying his best and never giving up, for the best celebrations on finishing his races, and for his friendly and outgoing manner. From Christopher, they learnt what true sportsmanship meant.

We loved watching Christopher as he learnt to swim and joined the swimming club with his siblings. He enjoyed ten-pin bowling, tennis and basketball. We somehow managed to make all the weekend sporting commitments with him and his brother, who also tried cricket, basketball and soccer on top of swimming and athletics, and his sister, who also did dance on top of everything else. Christopher drained us just as much as his siblings did in getting him to all of his weekend sporting commitments.

We loved seeing the relationship with his little brother grow, except he is not so little anymore. The bond they have is unbreakable, and it is on show for the world to see as we eagerly plan for Daniel's wedding and Christopher's best man's speech. Equally, we loved watching his excitement as he welcomed his little sister into our family and watching him cheer the loudest every time she performed in a dance concert on the stage.

When you have a child with a disability, too often, you are portrayed as a martyr, as suffering from the burden of having a child with a disability. Too often, the sheer joy of having a child is overshadowed and lost. Too often, we just see a child with a disability for the burden they bring rather than the joy, happiness and the learning they bring to a family. Yes, caring is a difficult job. It is a lifetime commitment, far more involved than it is for your other children, and yes, sometimes it is lonely, frustrating, and hard. But our amazing little family is so amazing because we have Christopher in it. From Christopher, we have all learnt so much.

From Christopher, we have all learnt humility. We have learnt acceptance, acceptance of people for who they are, and acceptance of the vast diversity of our population. Everyone in our family are quite happy to speak to anyone with a disability if they want to interact with us. Too often, we see people that Christopher tries to interact with not know what to say, or what to do. Just be yourself, respond, acknowledge, and greet them as you would anyone else. Christopher's brother and sister have always interacted naturally with anyone and accept everyone's natural right to be included in all aspects of society.

From Christopher, we have learnt patience, both patience for what we want to achieve and patience to try and understand what he is saying, what he wants and what he needs. Learning for Christopher has always been difficult, and it still is, but he still tries. Communicating is especially difficult, but Christopher tries hard and has learnt many other ways of communicating using augmentative and alternative communication.

Sometimes Christopher would say something, and I would not understand it, but Daniel or Stephanie would, and they were proud to be able to translate. While we are often impatient to achieve what we want to do, Christopher has taught us that not everything is easy and that sometimes we just have to try harder.

From Christopher, we have learnt kindness and compassion. I remember one day, I was at a Special Kids Christmas party, a large charity event for disadvantaged chidren and children with disabilities, sponsored by 4KQ, a local Brisbane radio station. We were just sitting down at the end of the day, having a drink before we left to go home. Nearby was another younger boy with Down syndrome who started crying because he lost his helium balloon. Christopher immediately jumped up and ran over with his balloon to give to the little boy. Both the other mum and I had tears in our eyes to see such caring and compassion.

Christopher has taught us to be open and honest with our feelings. The absolute joy on his face when opening his presents at his 18th birthday party was something that the staff at the little restaurant that we booked were amazed at. The owner told me that the staff enjoyed working that shift to see the natural expression of joy from Christopher and his friends as they celebrated his birthday.

Being open and honest with our feelings is something that we have all learnt from Christopher, and it is something that many people can learn from interacting with our son. And yes, we know when he is upset too, he definitely lets us know, and equally, we know when he is sorry if he has upset us.

As a family, Christopher has brought us much joy, and we have all learnt so much from him. He has shaped the people we are today. Christopher's younger brother, Daniel, is a support worker and draws on his experience of growing up with his brother to support his holistic model of support t empower his clients. Stephanie has just graduated from university as an Occupational Therapist. Her experiences have developed her empathy, a vital skill in her career path.

However, I would like to return to my first thoughts when he was born. Did having Christopher impact the plan that I had for my life? Was I able to achieve everything that I had planned before he was born? Or did my role as a carer impact that plan?

Having Christopher did change my plans a little, and it certainly influenced them a lot. Before he was born, I was contemplating further study in either special education or guidance counselling. Having Christopher cemented my idea for further study in special education. After completing this further study and working as a special education teacher in a couple of different high schools, I went to a presentation about some research being conducted at the University of Queensland.

The research was about developing the literacy skills of adults with Down syndrome. I decided I wanted more. With Christopher as my inspiration, I went on to research developing numeracy in adults with Down syndrome and other intellectual disabilities in both a masters and PhD. I began working as a casual lecturer at a couple of different universities educating teachers on becoming the inclusive educators of tomorrow. Having completed my PhD, I have secured a permanent position at a university and am continuing to research in the areas of mathematics for students who struggle and ways of supporting inclusive education.

Having Christopher has inspired my future career rather than stifled it. He has been the inspiration for my further study, my research, and for my career. This is my story, and I am certain it is different to your story, but aren't all our stories of family life different? Aren't all our experiences with all of our children different? If you are reading this as a new parent of a child with a disability, whether that child is a newborn or an older child with a new diagnosis, you might be thinking that your situation is different, and my experience does not mean anything in your context. I would agree with that thought, but I do have some advice for you.

Right back when my son was born, I had a visit from another young mum who had a child with Down syndrome. I asked that mum if she went back to work after her son was born. She said, 'No, but I never intended to go back to work. I wanted to be a stay-at-home mum, and that is what I have done. But that is what I always intended to do. If you want to go back to work, then do that. You should always do what you intend to do. It might not quite be the same, but you can do it; you might just need to reimagine how that looks'.

For me, being a school teacher, going back to work was not too difficult. We had daycare, and I had school holidays off. When my children were at school, I was at work. Although, as any teacher will tell you, we do a heap of work during the school holidays, but time was flexible, and I was able to make it work. Things became more challenging when Christopher left school, as daycare clearly wasn't an option and funding for support was extremely scarce. Setting up appropriate, meaningful, and purposeful activities was certainly challenging at a time when many day services operated similarly to daycare centres.

By this time, I had started working casually at university and had cut down on my days at school. Soon I cut out school teaching altogether, focused on casual work at university and began my PhD. Managing this time was challenging and required financial support towards the cost of Christopher's care, but with the advent of the NDIS, his care needs were catered for. However, the challenge of finding inspiring staff and setting up the team of support workers that I have was difficult but rewarding. Christopher now does a variety of activities from delivering the local paper, helping at the library, volunteering at a number of charity shops and local businesses, as well as hosting a zoom cooking class once a week with his friends.

My advice to new parents is to explore the new opportunities that present themselves with the realisation that your child has a disability. Explore other ways of achieving the life goals that you already had in mind, and be open to the new possibilities that life presents. Think of what you can learn from your child and what value your child brings to your family, for you, and for all members of your family.

# Life In The Fast Lane

## Chris Hill

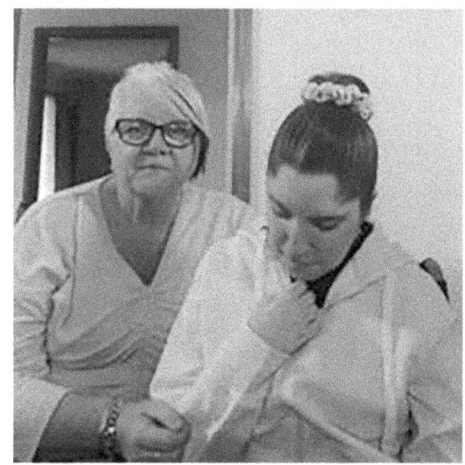

Let me introduce myself. My name is Chris Hill, and my journey includes my husband and our three girls, Bridgett and her siblings, Angela and Belinda. Bridgett, our youngest, now 29 years old, was born with a disability. My story begins in brief like this.

The first twelve months were about fighting for answers, admissions to the hospital and so forth. Crying and, dare I say, begging for help. There was something wrong, Bridgett was our third child, and we knew things weren't right.

Finally, after many tears and many sleepless nights and following a major procedure at six months old and many more appointments, it was confirmed that Bridgett was born with a disability. It was lifelong, and the impact on her life would be significant.

Our gut instinct was confirmed, and it was onward and upwards from that day. We took on every opportunity and engaged in all supports offered that would help our young girl and help us gain knowledge about her disability.

We also had two other children, Angela and Belinda, to look after and, at the time, were self-employed. It was hard, and we did cry some tears, that's for sure. At the time, my dad had dementia. Some days, my mum and I would just sit there watching the pair of them, one in his wheelchair and the other in her pram, both of us knowing our lives had definitely changed.

I remember reading the poem, *Welcome to Holland* by Emily Perl Kingsley. I must have read this about 100 times over the next few years. In short, it was my therapy. I would like to share it here:

### Welcome to Holland

*When you're going to have a baby, it's like you're planning a vacation to Italy. You're all excited. You get a whole bunch of guidebooks, you learn a few phrases so you can get around, and then it comes time to pack your bags and head for the airport.*

*Only when you land, the stewardess says, 'WELCOME TO HOLLAND.'*

*You look at one another in disbelief and shock, saying, 'HOLLAND? WHAT ARE YOU TALKING ABOUT? I SIGNED UP FOR ITALY.'*

*But they explain that there's been a change of plan, that you've landed in Holland and there you must stay.*

*'BUT I DON'T KNOW ANYTHING ABOUT HOLLAND!' you say. 'I DON'T WANT TO STAY!'*

*But stay, you do.*

*You go out and buy some new guidebooks, you learn some new phrases, and you meet people you never knew existed.*

*The important thing is that you are not in a bad place filled with despair. You're simply in a different place than you had planned.*

*It's slower paced than Italy, less flashy than Italy, but after you've been there a little while and you have a chance to catch your breath, you begin to discover that Holland has windmills. Holland has tulips. Holland has Rembrandts.*

*But everyone else you know is busy coming and going from Italy. They're all bragging about what a great time they had there, and for the rest of your life, you'll say, 'YES, THAT'S WHAT I HAD PLANNED.'*

*The pain of that will never go away.*

*You have to accept that pain, because the loss of that dream, the loss of that plan, is a very, very significant loss.*

*But if you spend your life mourning the fact that you didn't get to go to Italy, you will never be free to enjoy the very special, the very lovely things about Holland.*

The important thing was our house was full of love as we processed what was happening.

By the time Bridgett had started school, I had five years of being a carer. I was already on the committee for a state-of-the-art, purpose built. Kindergarten. I joined the parent group at the special school and was on the school board.

I wanted the best for our girl, and this I felt was a way of contributing. Meanwhile, hubby would take Belinda to modelling, and I would take Angela to Netball, while surviving this new adventure in our life.

I, like the poem says, met new friends, became an advocate for all and quietly cried at night while putting a smile on my dial for the new day.

When Bridgett was settled in school, I started volunteering, which then led to study and full-time employment. You guessed it! Carer support. I got to support other carers helping them along the way. My girls, through my work, enjoyed being supported as young carers. Again, knowing that I was not always there for them or could not always listen when they needed me another passion of mine was to make sure that they were supported in enjoying camps and outings as young carers and hopefully not feeling alone during this journey. This was our way of making sure and a way of saying thank you for helping and being great kids.

I remained in that job for 20 years until 2019. Life was okay, and we were managing.

Then at the age of 10 years, I remember the day like it was yesterday. Bridgett was looking very tired and black around the eyes, and within an hour of noticing, Bridgett had been rushed to Intensive care and was diagnosed with Type one Diabetes. This day was like someone saying to us, 'Well, you two, I can see you're both coping, so here's another blow to your life in the fast lane.'

This was a new chapter of our caring journey. Our world again, as we knew it, had been rocked. Again, our other girls were on the back burner while we supported and struggled with the news of Bridgett's latest diagnosis.

Bridgett was nonverbal, needed a wheelchair outside of the home, and lived with severe reflux and severe arthritis in both knees. Doubly incontinent, so Type One was, for us, devastating, a new level of care. I remember being asked once, 'If you had one wish, what would it be?' I said, 'I wish Bridgett didn't have diabetes'. Then I laughed to myself as I hadn't wished that Bridgett didn't have a disability, just that she didn't diabetes. We were doing okay life was different, but it was good, rocky, scary, and yes, it threw us.

Bridgett was 17 years of age when she was officially diagnosed with Pitt Hopkins Syndrome. I remember that also as another huge moment. So the diagnosis was given, and in a moment, I felt closure. We knew what Bridgett's disability was. I even said to the paediatrician, because 17 years on you learnt to have a sense of humour, that, 'I'm going to call it Pitt Hopkins Disability.' He responded, 'Okay, why's that?' And me being me, said, 'Well, I have always wanted a child with a PHD.' Yes, we even bought the T-SHIRT.

Meanwhile, while living our best life, our two oldest girls were growing up before our eyes. I will always feel that they only got part of me while they grew. I wish I could have given more of the real me and not the tired, scared and worried mum. I have cried many tears for them. Before I knew it, they were grown and had left home. Both became young mums at an early age.

Eighteen years on, however, they are very much beautiful mums and with their partners still, and I have a total of eight grandchildren between them. They both work in disability and are the best mum's ever. My husband and I could not be prouder. We have a wonderful and close relationship with them all and are very blessed.

Today, Bridgett is 29 years old and will be turning the big 30 in June. Her health is declining, and her ability to weight bare is extremely poor. We are investigating what this will look like for her, for us as carers, and for life in general. I want to cry, but I can't, and I feel grateful for having her on her feet for nearly 30 years. I am grateful that my babe still is with us, as we have had many scares over the years.

She has been on life support more times than I care to think about.

Bridgett today, apart from her Pitt Hopkins Syndrome, has osteoarthritis, and she lives with reflux.

Bridgett is nonverbal, doubly incontinent with PMDD related to PMS. She has Type one diabetes, so is insulin dependent. She has an Intellectual disability and requires full support for all personal care and is now looking at scoliosis of the spine. But apart from all of that, Bridgett is fine. On a good day, she is hard work, if I'm honest.

There are days when I could run away, but then I say I can't because she needs feeding or pc done or fed. These thoughts come and go for a split second, maybe at 3 am in the morning when I am changing bedding, dealing with a hypo or hyper. When I want to nip to the shops but can't, or if I do, I need a nappy/pad, jelly beans, wheelchair, bag, everything in case! In case we break down, in case who knows, but there is no just nipping out.

I get sad as I can't just go to my girls' homes for a visit. Lucky for us, our girls are wonderful and pop in most weeks. They both work, and I babysit when possible, but they have never put pressure on me, and I love who they are.

Bridgett, well, she let me share. She is feisty, cheeky, funny, loud, a bit like her mother, and enjoys it when someone is in trouble. She can clear a room very quickly. Bridgett is a grabber who scratches and has a Positive Behaviour Support plan in place. We now have restrictive practices removed so we're doing well. That's thanks to the NDIS.

Bridgett has choices. We help her with them, support with working what's best for her, and are able to have funding for all to happen. Bridgett has her respite in a very fancy hotel, purpose-built, and she thinks she's it when staying with her 24-hour supports. She doesn't go with strangers. She goes with her girlfriend, who she started school with, and now they go to Day Options together.

We have never thought about what Bridgett can't do. We say that at 29, she has the right to do different things. She has been put on swings, planes, boats, rides, you name it, and has been going to respite for weekends for a very long time. Bridgett has a great life. She is getting some grey hair, and we laughingly say to her, 'Not sure why you have the grey hair because we do all the work.' My husband and I are not getting any younger. I am about to turn 61, and he is 68; I'm not sure when that happened, but it has.

As all carers, if I could share anything, it would be, 'It's okay to be happy and positive.'

Yes, on our journey , we do think about when we are not here. I think all parents do, but in particular, you think about this when you have a child with a disability; what that will look like, and with who or where will they live when you are no longer there.

At the moment, well, this week anyway, Bridgett lives at home. What I am sure of is that we have, and I feel very happy with our choices in doing so, is that we have prepared our youngest by introducing her to changes for days without us, with holidays and weekends away. Was it perfect? No. Did we have hiccups? Yes. However, life has that anyway, disability or not.

Bridgett has limited communication and is nonverbal, but believe me, she can get a message across and, at 29, continues to show us that she is still learning. We are still excited, and we never say never. We say it may not happen overnight, but it could happen.

We pick our battles; we don't want her to do everything, and we want to be happy. We have also shared with her siblings and made it very clear from an early that they are not responsible for caring for Bridgett as adults. They are her advocates, her siblings, and her family. Bridgett, however, needs support 24/7 and we would love for them to be with her in life on a happy level.

Both my husband and I still work, and this keeps us busy and allows me to have a purpose for myself. I love going to work. I love supporting other carers. I love being a part of the journey, the journey we didn't plan.

Yes, at times I get jealous and wish I could go here, there and everywhere at the drop of a hat, but mostly we're good.

I would like to share *Celebrating Holland – I'm Home*, by Cathy Anthony, in response to the poem, *Welcome to Holland*, as I feel the same way:

*I have been in Holland for over a decade now. It has become home. I have had time to catch my breath, to settle and adjust, to accept something different than I'd planned. I reflect back on those years of past when I had first landed in Holland. I remember clearly my shock, my fear, my anger, the pain and uncertainty. In those first few years, I tried to get back to Italy as planned, but Holland was where I was to stay. Today, I can say how far I have come on this unexpected journey. I have learned so much more. But, this too has been a journey of time.*

*I worked hard. I bought new guidebooks. I learned a new language and I slowly found my way around this new land. I have met others whose plans had changed like mine, and who could share my experience. We supported one another and some have become very special friends. Some of these fellow travellers had been in Holland longer than I and were seasoned guides, assisting me along the way. Many have encouraged me. Many have taught me to open my eyes to the wonder and gifts to behold in this new land. I have discovered a community of caring. Holland wasn't so bad.*

*I think that Holland is used to wayward travellers like me and grew to become a land of hospitality, reaching out to welcome, to assist and to support newcomers like me in this new land. Over the years, I've wondered what life would have been like if I'd landed in Italy as planned. Would life have been easier? Would it have been as rewarding? Would I have learned some of the important lessons I hold today?*

*Sure, this journey has been more challenging and at times I would (and still do) stomp my feet and cry out in frustration and protest. And, yes, Holland is slower paced than Italy and less flashy than Italy, but this too has been an unexpected gift. I have learned to slow down in ways too and look closer at things, with a new appreciation for the remarkable beauty of Holland with its tulips, windmills and Rembrandts.*

*I have come to love Holland and call it Home. I have become a world traveller and discovered that it doesn't matter where you land. What's more important is what you make of your journey and how you see and enjoy the very special, the very lovely, things that Holland, or any land, has to offer.*

*Yes, over a decade ago I landed in a place I hadn't planned. Yet I am thankful, for this destination has been richer than I could have imagined!*

So in closing, I hope you enjoyed reading about our babe, our girl, our rascal. Because we truly are enjoying having her in our lives.

We are the lucky ones, as I truly believe we are much better people for having Bridgett in our lives.

One tired, happy mum

Chris Hill

# The Authors and Bios

From Left:

*Top Row:* Christine Stow, Jenny Nechvatal, Julie Fisher, Nicole Dunn

*Middle Row:* Chris Hill, Anastasia Searle, Lorraine Gaunt

*Bottom Row:* Alessandra Pelletier, Monique Peters, Irina Castellano, Graciela Ramon Michel

# Christine Stow

Author
Speaker
Winner: International Stevie Women in Silver Business Award.
Former Local Councillor
Empowered Women in Business: Founder.

Life was going well for Christine, from working in Forensic Laboratory to moving into Medical and Laboratory sales. She became the State Sales Manager for a Laboratory Supply company and tripled sales turnover. Then as a Medical National Technical Adviser for a Medical Supplier, she was flying all around the country and internationally, but when she found something wrong with her daughter at three months of age, she had to reinvent herself. Since then, she has completed an MBA, stood in a State Election, was elected to council, set up a special school and a café for people with disabilities and stood in the Federal Election against the opposition leader of the Country.

From carer to councillor, she is a master of reinvention who has set up projects from concept - from an idea in someone's mind to reality- projects such as a Holiday Program for Children with disabilities, which has a turnover in the $100,000s of Dollars Proposition, a Special School, to a Café that people with disabilities run. These are just a few of the projects Christine has brought to fruition. And she is not finished yet.

Now she helps women to find their true gifts, and realise their value so that they can bring an income to live the life of their dreams. 'We owe it to ourselves to step into OUR GREATNESS & we all have something to offer.' she says.

www.christinestow.com.au

Phone: +61 439385217

Facebook: https://www.facebook.com/christine.stow.1

Facebook Page: https://www.facebook.com/ChristineAStow/

# Irina Castellano

Irina Castellano is an authorised foster carer who is dedicated to providing safe homes for vulnerable children, especially now that we have hundreds of kids sitting in motel rooms as we do not have enough safe homes for them to go to.

Her work has been featured in a dozen podcasts, three books, articles, as well as radio interviews with *SBS German Radio* and *The Meaningful Monday Radio Show*. She also runs the nationally accredited Foster Carer Programs and Adoption seminars.

Using her over twenty years of experience, Irina provides awareness and education about all aspects of fostering. She offers professional one-on-one support, training and guidance to all potential foster carers and hopeful adoptive parents.

Along with her husband and three children, Irina has provided a home to over eighty children. Her upcoming memoir will cover her life as an ex-pat in eight countries and her honest account of her foster and adoptive journey.

Irina is a co-author in a book. This is the link: www.elevatebooks.com/performance

If you are interested in Irina's free eBook on fostering/adoption, please send her an email:

irina@irinacastellano.com.au

If you would like to listen to my podcast no. 57: elevatebooks.com/category/podcast/

The fellow co-author, Alessandra Pelletier, is her sister.

# Nicole Dunn

Nicole Dunn is a qualified Physiotherapist and Care Coordinator with over 17 years of experience in the healthcare sector. Nicole was inspired to be an advocate for older people after becoming a live-in carer for her Nanna, who was diagnosed with terminal pancreatic cancer.

In 2015, Nicole founded Empower Aged Care Consulting, a purposed-based business focused on assisting older people to navigate My Aged Care as their representative. Nicole's passion lies at a grassroots level by drawing on personal experiences and industry knowledge to help older people age well in their own home by improving access to home care services.

In 2019, Nicole was an expert witness at the Australian Royal Commission into Aged Care Quality and Safety, speaking about her experience as a carer. Nicole's industry knowledge and compassion make her a sought-after aged care commentator.

Empower Aged Care Consulting

www.empoweragecare.com.au

# Julie Fisher

Julie Fisher is wife to Mick, Mum to Caleb, Blake and Darcy, Step mum to Bree, and she is also a carer for her son Darcy.

After completing her dream of writing her first book, *The Unexpected Journey: Embracing the Beauty of Disability*, a burning passion was ignited to do more within the Down Syndrome community and also for others living with a disability.

Since completing her first book, Julie has worked together with other disability groups, such as Down Syndrome Australia and Down Syndrome Victoria, and has been part of the Truly Incredible Care Campaign in 2020 with Carers Victoria.

She has published a second book titled *The Magic of Inclusion, Give People A Chance And Watch Them Shine* and recently published her third book titled *From The Hearts of Mums, Stories of Love and Inclusion in the World of Down Syndrome*.

She has written many articles which have been published on media platforms online as well as realising another dream of doing a TedX Talk, and she is now the host of a local radio show titled *The Unexpected Journey*.

Julie recently hosted her first local disability expo, and she has spoken about her journey with her son Darcy in the hope of raising awareness in the wider community as well as helping other families.

She has also become a voice in the Carer community and has worked with Carers Victoria as a facilitator with online workshops, a panel member on discussion boards, an ambassador for National Carers Week and with her son Darcy, has been part of two campaigns with them.

Julie's hope is for everyone to be treated fairly and the same, and to enjoy life's adventures.

Follow Julie at:

https://www.facebook.com/theunexpectedjourneybook

Website -www.juliefisher.com.au

# Lorraine Gaunt

Originally beginning her career as a mathematics and science teacher in Queensland secondary schools, the birth of her first child with Down syndrome inspired Lorraine to further study, completing a Graduate Diploma in Special Education, Masters of Philosophy in mathematics education for adults with Down syndrome, and a PhD in supporting numeracy development for adults with intellectual disability.

Dr Lorraine Gaunt is a Lecturer of Education in the School of Education at Charles Sturt University. Lorraine completed her PhD at the University of Queensland in 2020 on the topic of supporting numeracy for adults with intellectual disability. She has over 25 years experience as a Secondary Mathematics and Special Education teacher and Head of Special Education Services at a range of Queensland secondary schools, and 12 years experience working in the tertiary education sector, previously working at both the University of Southern Queensland and the University of Queensland.

Lorraine's research interests include supporting numeracy development and promoting inclusive mathematics education in the secondary classroom. Additionally, Lorraine is passionate about improving the wellbeing of individuals with disabilities and promoting inclusive communities.

Lorraine was awarded the Early Career Award for her research paper and presentation at the 2022 Mathematics Education Research Group of Australasia (MERGA) conference in Tasmania.

https://arts-ed.csu.edu.au/schools/education/staff/profiles/teaching-and-research-staff/dr-lorraine-gaunt

https://orcid.org/0000-0003-4835-3414

LinkedIn: https://www.linkedin.com/in/lorraine-gaunt-5b130837/

# Chris Hill

Chris is employed as a Family and Carer Liaison for Novita, based in Adelaide. She works 35 hours a week, and this keeps her connected to a world outside of her caring role.

Chris was born in Northern Ireland Belfast, and came to Australia as a child back in 1968, and it wasn't until 2019 that she returned as an adult. It was an experience she will always remember and will do again.

Chris went to a good old public school, back in the day when you would get the cane if you misbehaved. Prior to being a parent of a person with a disability, Chris worked as a self-employed contractor for housing.

Chris' personal life changed, and therefore, her goals in life changed. She needed to improve her child's life and ensure she received the best life possible. Her professional goals changed, her thirst for learning changed, and she desired to be the best she could be on this unexpected journey. Chris volunteered, studied, and found a niche for life that she never knew she could. Her role also was to make sure her child was supported and that her siblings were included and not excluded. She started a job in Carer Support and has remained in that role for over 25 years. She still sings on her way to work, and feels good.

Chris regards her achievements and accomplishments as still being happily married, and having children who are happy, independent young women, with strength of their own. Chris still has one young lady at home, and Chris is focusing on preparing her daughter for the world without her.

Chris doesn't worry about what she can't change. She has learnt to pick her battles, and most importantly, she is happy and proud of herself.

Her hobbies - well, without giving too much away, she loves a good party, loves girls' weekends away, and weekends away with other carers and couples. She loves a good pub, old music and songs you can sing to.

Chris is juggling this life we call normal and continuing to 'never say never' and is always prepared to learn, listen, never judge and support another.

# Jenny Nechvatal

Jenny Nechvatal is a mother of three children, two of whom are living with a disability. She currently runs her business, Innovate Support Coordination. Prior to this, Jenny was an Early Childhood teacher with over 30 years of experience in the early childhood sector.

The experience of being a parent, her workplace experiences within the early childhood sector, and her experience as a support coordinator, advocating for individuals living with a disability, has shaped Jenny's direction.

Jenny hopes to support families and early childhood educators to better understand the experience of families living with a diagnosis. Jenny aims to achieve this by providing insight and offering solutions on how to manage the everyday aspects of supporting those living with a disability and their support unit.

This is something Jenny is extremely passionate about. It is rewarding to observe the abilities of these children, through the implementation of strategies allowing each child to reach their full potential.

**Innovate Support Coordination**
Phone: +61 447 604 180
https://www.innovatesupportcoordination.org
https://www.facebook.com/supportandcoordination

**Innovative Disability Solutions**
https://innovativedisabilitysolutions.squarespace.com/
**Instagram:**@innovativedisabilitysolutions
**Facebook:** Innovative Disability Solutions
https://www.facebook.com/profile.php?id=100089426503616

# Alessandra Pelletier

Growing up in different parts of the world, (France, USA Germany, & Turkey) sparked Alessandra's interest to pursue foreign language studies, but once she met her American husband, Jeff, during his military duty in Germany, her plans took a rather different turn.

As a nanny in France, Alessandra had proclaimed that she'd never have kids, and a big family wasn´t Jeff´s original plan either. He had wanted one child only. They were married within a year, and as the first child was born, they definitely changed their opinion on the subject of family size.

Even though the birth of their firstborn wasn´t an easy undertaking, the midwife told Alessandra that one day she would give birth to a total of 12 kids!

She must have had some accurate intuition, as they eventually had 11 kids (the firstborn was a twin, but the twin was lost during the early stage of the pregnancy).

They are very grateful for each and every child and their unique personalities. Though they definitely had their struggles, Alessandra loved being a stay-at-home mum. At the time of writing, there are only three children still left at home in Germany, including Justin, and they have five grandchildren so far as well.

The fellow co-author, Irina Castellano, is her sister.

# Monique Peters

Monique is a mum in greater western Sydney, who is on a mission to increase awareness about auditory processing disorder (APD), the role it plays in learning challenges and how neuroscience can physically improve a brain's ability to learn.

Her son's academic and social challenges at school motivated her, and on the journey, she found hope in a book called *The Brain That Changes Itself* by Dr Norman Doidge. Monique later supported several families working with a forward-thinking speech pathologist on Sydney's north shore who used an evidence-based, neuroscience program to strengthen the learning pathways in the brain. Impressed with the results, Monique soon developed a vision for helping other mums in greater western Sydney.

In 2018, Monique started her business without, however, the skills to reach her audience. So she used the growth mindset strategies she learned to support her students to develop her own skillset. Everything from how to handle the imposter syndrome she feels as a mum talking publicly about neuroscience to mastering accounting and the finer points of trademarking for the launch of her new program *Learnerobics*™.

Her son Lincoln, now 21, has now joined her in the business. As a field rep, Lincoln hits the streets and talks to people about APD and how it can be improved with the *Learnerobics*™ program. He is also using his social media marketing skills to boost her audience reach.

Looking forward, Brain Wise Learning hopes to open more doors for children and adults with learning challenges, with or without a diagnosis.

People make use of the programs at Brain Wise Learning to improve their attention, memory, language reading and learning mindset.

If you would like to connect with Monique, her details are:
https://www.facebook.com/brainwiselearningaus/
https://www.linkedin.com/in/monique-peters-learning/
https://www.pinterest.com.au/imalearning2/
https://www.instagram.com/brainwiselearning
https://www.youtube.com/@brainwiselearningaustralia

# Graciela Ramon Michel

Graciela is the founder of Graceful Coaching.

Her purpose and mission are to guide and support parents of children with special needs. These are parents who are overwhelmed, exhausted, and stressed.

Graciela's parenting support methods stem directly from her own life experience as a single working mother in Argentina raising two sons, one of whom is severely autistic. She now lives in Australia, where she relocated from Argentina in 2001 with her husband Daniel and daughter Camille, while her two sons, Martin and Federico, remained in Argentina. Federico, Graciela's second son, has blessed her life with two beautiful granddaughters, Sofia and Martina.

The defining moment of Graciela's life came to her as a serious question. After years of pushing herself to the breaking point, she developed pancreatitis for no apparent reason other than stress and was admitted to intensive care. Her doctor asked her if she wanted to live, and she had a realization at this moment. Her answer was, 'Yes, because I love my children and I love myself'. This brought Graciela back from the brink of despair and changed her perception of the challenges she was facing in her life and her desire to seek support for them. She realised that in order to be present for her children, she needed to be present for herself first.

Graciela's approach guides parents through a sequence of realizations that help in the development of compassion for themselves and their children. She has created and delivered a series of online workshops with Moira, a non-profit health organization that establishes a gentle conversation with parents. This provides them with an opportunity to explore with a sense of peace and clarity, defining them as individuals as well as parents. From this perspective, they can find a personal determination to approach things with greater clarity and love, and they are less influenced by the external chaos and uncertainty that accompany the challenges of raising a special needs child.

With her support and guidance, parents find a renewed zest and appreciation for life that will sustain them through the ongoing challenges with a critical difference, which is what leads to a path of healing and reconnection. This difference is a change of mindset that recognises prior challenges as opportunities for growth in love for themselves and their children.

Unleash your inner power and create strong bonds with your children to begin flourishing in your life with them. Connect with Graciela at: graciela@gracefulcoaching.me

Facebook:
https://www.facebook.com/gracefulcoaching.me
Instagram:
https://www.instagram.com/grace.fulcoaching/

For more information, visit her LinkedIn at: https://www.linkedin.com/in/graciela-ramon-michel/

# Anastasia Searle

Anastasia has a daughter with a disability so she understands this challenging and complex journey, and that is why she loves what she does!

Anastasia has nearly 20 years experience in the mindset & disability industries and is the owner of Bloom Networking.

Anastasia and her team offer Support Co-Ordination, Psychosocial Recovery and Mindset programs for NDIS participants and for people with a disability. The journey in pivoting her business to include disability programs was one Anastasia fought for a long time due to her own situation raising a child with a disability, but that divine nudge was relentless. She now whole-heartedly embraces the opportunity and has seen lives changed.

Anastasia is a highly trained, experienced and sought-after mindset trainer, coach and public speaker. She has worked with nearly 8,000 people during her career running mindset programs, networking events, awards and one-on-one coaching.

Through her mindset programs and coaching, Anastasia specialises in helping people implement strategies to create rapid positive outcomes in their lives.

Her influence has been impactful and far-reaching. She has had public speaking opportunities both in person and online, spreading her inspiring message.

# Other Books By The Authors

# Not Just Imyjen's Mother
## Christine Stow

My First book, *Not Just Imyjen's Mother*, was a watershed for me since it was the first time I'd ever left Imyjen alone for more than three hours.

It made me realise that anything is possible if you believe you can.

Through writing this book, I share my journey from finding something wrong with Imyjen, on how I overcame the challenges to stand up and speak for others.

If there is a message that I want readers to take away is that there is so much to be had if we embrace the journey to feel the love and joy.

# The Unexpected Journey
## Julie Fisher

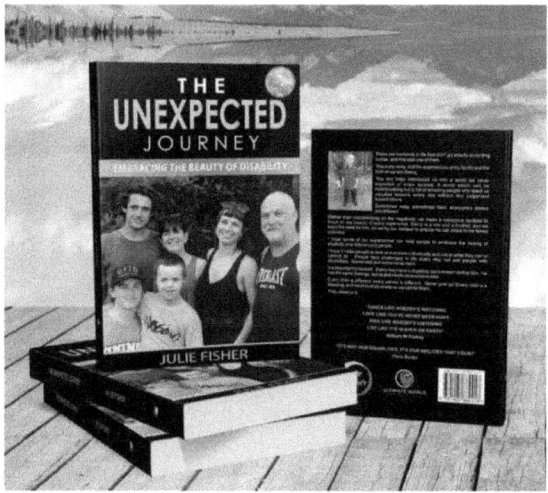

There are moments in life that don't go exactly according to plan, and this was one of them.

*The Unexpected Journey* is Julie's story, and the experiences of her family and the birth of their son Darcy.

Their tiny baby introduced them into a world they never expected or knew existed. A world which can be heartbreaking but is full of amazing people who teach us valuable lessons every day without any judgement toward others.

Rather than concentrating on the negatives, they made a conscious decision to focus on the beauty of every experience. Darcy is a son and a brother, and we want the best for him, so we try our hardest to ensure he can shine to his fullest potential.

Follow Julie here

https://www.facebook.com/theunexpectedjourneybook

# The Magic Of Inclusion
## Julie Fisher

Inclusion isn't something that anyone should have to fight for – but for many, this is an everyday battle that feels like it will never end.

Have you ever thought what it would be like if your child, or someone you care for, was made to feel like they shouldn't be somewhere or shouldn't do something that others take for granted? If you took your child to a play centre, park or the movies and they were excluded by others, just because they looked or behaved differently?

In this inspiring book, Julie shares real-life stories that demonstrate why we must promote inclusion not just in groups, clubs, and organisations, but also in our everyday interactions with others. *The Magic of Inclusion* shows us how the simple act of including others can be life-changing.

Follow Julie here
https://www.facebook.com/theunexpectedjourneybook

# From the Heart of Mums
## Julie Fisher

When you enter the world of disability with your child or anyone you care for, it can be a scary time of the unknown. Your idea of what life was going to be like suddenly changes in an instant.

In this heartwarming book, Julie Fisher shares 13 deeply personal stories from mums around the world of their lives with loved ones who live with Down syndrome.

You will discover how these mums navigated the path from diagnosis to present day, and how with love and guidance, this new world of disability has led them into a world of support from people they never imagined possible.

These inspiring stories from the hearts of mums show the true beauty of disability, and how embracing it helps us all to shine.

Follow Julie here
https://www.facebook.com/theunexpectedjourneybook